# ELEMENTARY
# Grammar

# ELEMENTARY Grammar

## A Child's Resource Book

## by Carl B. Smith, Ph.D.

GRAYSON BERNARD
PUBLISHERS

*Printed in the United States of America*

**Publisher's Cataloging in Publication Data**
*(Prepared by Quality Books Inc.)*

Smith, Carl Bernard, 1932-
   Elementary grammar: a child's resource book / by Carl B. Smith.--
p. cm. -- (Using your language series.)
   Includes index and answer key to exercises.
   ISBN 0-9628556-2-6


   1. English language -- Grammar.    I. Title.  II. Series.

PE1111          425         91-73873

*Book & cover design by Addie Seabarkrob*

Grayson Bernard Publishers
223 S. Pete Ellis Dr., Suite 12
Bloomington, Indiana 47408

# Contents

# Detailed Table of Contents

# Detailed Table of Contents

# Detailed Table of Contents

# A Word to Parents

Thank you for showing an interest in your child's language development. Skill in using the English language marks the person who cares about clear thought and about communicating with others. With this book, you and your child have a resource that will answer questions about language, grammar, and punctuation.

*Elementary Grammar* is written for children who are in their early years in school. It covers the material that is usually presented in the study of language in the first four grades. In this book you will find answers to these questions:

- How is the English language organized?
- How can we understand the parts of speech and the ways they relate to one another?
- How can a knowledge of English help us speak and write clearly and correctly?

This book is meant to serve as a **reference source** and a **handbook** that complements the instruction usually given in school. It is not a textbook and is not designed to replace work done in the classroom. This book provides review and additional practice for students who may need such study. It also allows younger students to move ahead and to explore topics that may not be covered in their textbooks.

Although it is not intended to be an activities book, *Elementary Grammar* does contain some practice questions in the "Check Your Understanding" sections at the end of each chapter. These exercises allow students to see how well they understand the material given in each chapter. If any exercises cause problems, then they indicate which material should be reviewed. These exercises will be especially helpful to children whose schools no longer teach grammar and punctuation directly.

This is a **resource book,** much like a dictionary or an encyclopedia. It should be used selectively to suit the age and the needs of each student. Younger children may need to study only portions of each chapter; parental help will be especially appropriate here. Older students may want to study entire chapters, or they may

# A Word to Parents

use the Index and then consult specific definitions and examples within each chapter. They can also turn directly to the Handbook to find concise information about individual topics when this best serves their needs.

If you want to use this book more formally, you will find each chapter organized in ways that require your child to *think* about how English sentences are constructed. The purpose is to help children draw their own conclusions. You can work with your child, if you wish, and answer any questions that may arise.

Although younger children will probably need parental help, most students in the third and fourth grades should be able to read and understand the material for themselves. Even so, parents can help children understand how to use the Index, to find things that are listed there, and to locate material in the Handbook.

If you do work with your child, try to make each session brief and light. Points of grammar and puctuation are best learned over time and with constant repetition. Keep study sessions short and frequent.

In the early stages of writing, young children are concerned only with expresssing themselves. They write in much the same way they speak, as this example from the early second grade shows:

> I have a dog his name is Fred and I have a cat his name is Max and another cat his name is Bubbles.

As they grow older, children become more and more sophisticated in their writing. When they begin to put their thoughts into more complicated sentences, they often run into problems such as those found in the next example, written by a student near the end of the second grade:

> We had a picnic outside we had realy food it was good because it tast fine.

Even though they can express complex ideas in speech, children need to learn that the reader must be considered when these ideas are written down. When younger students realize the importance of writing so that *others* can understand how their sentences are organized, then they will benefit most from this book.

Many of the examples in *Elementary Grammar* are taken directly from papers written by students in the early grades. This means that the book focuses on the topics that interest young children and on the problems they encounter as they learn to use the English language.

This book is organized for easy reference. Following a chapter on the sentence, there are chapters on the parts of speech that are usually discussed in the early grades: nouns, pronouns, verbs, adjectives, and adverbs. The chapter on Word Study helps your child understand how words are constructed, and the chapter on Writing Better Sentences deals with more elaborate sentence structures that students explore in the third and fourth grades. Punctuation is reviewed in the final chapter. Each chapter contains definitions, examples, more extensive discussion (where it is needed), and short practice exercises.

In the Handbook for Quick Reference, important topics are arranged in alphabetical order. Here the student will find brief definitions, along with examples. This handbook can be used to review information that has already been covered and to answer questions that may arise.

The Index provides an alphabetical listing of major topics (such as Nouns and Verbs) with subheads listed below each major topic. Furthermore, students will find that many of these subheads are also listed independently. For example, students can look under **Nouns** and then find the listing for **irregular plural nouns,** or they can look directly at the separate entry for **Irregular plural nouns.** Thus, students can learn how to find information *about* the English language while they are learning how to *use* that language.

As parents, you can help your child by encouraging and supporting the process of learning how to use the English language. Young children learn by attempting things that are beyond their level of ability, by making mistakes and persisting until they succeed. You can help by showing your child where to find the answers to questions that arise and by providing positive examples.

It is helpful to show children that a well-constructed sentence is clear and easy to understand. It is even more helpful to contrast such a sentence with another one that is not clear and correct. It is also desirable to show children that writing can and should involve revision: the first version of a sentence or a composition is only the starting point.

# A Word to Parents

Especially in the earliest grades, it is important not to point out every mistake but rather to stress only the most important things, such as the need for a subject and a verb in the sentence. Mistakes in spelling and grammar are necessary parts of the learning process and should be viewed positively. The important thing is for children to learn how to check for possible errors and where to find solutions to problems.

Learning what to do and what not to do can be a daunting experience for the young child, and he or she must be given time to master the intricacies of language. If you have never studied Greek or Russian or Chinese, then you might try to read or write a sentence in one of those languages. This will give you some idea of what young children are dealing with as they begin their study of the English language.

A student in the third grade wrote the following composition (printed here with a few minor adjustments):

> Doing things in school
> I like doing math and reading because it is fun. Math is neat because I'm good in multiplication and fractions. Reading is neat because I'm good at it. I like other things too like English, science, handwriting, and social studies. You learn a lot in them. Well, it is hard to do some of those things.

We hope that *Elementary Grammar* helps you to help your child "do some of those things" successfully.

# SENTENCES

## What is a sentence?

Do these groups of words make sense to you?

I like my teacher a lot. She is the best teacher in the whole solar system.

In our class we have two gerbils. Over the weekend one of the gerbils got out of the cage. We found her in the heater.

One day my sister tripped over a rock. The next day she tripped over a chair.

When I grow up I would like to study medicine. I would also like to give some riding lessons on different kinds of horses.

Have you seen the dinosaur bones in the museum? There were many kinds of dinosaurs. The meanest one was called Tyrannosaurus rex.

These are good sentences, and they were all written by students your age. They are clear and easy to understand. Each sentence makes sense when it is read by itself.

What is a sentence?

- A **sentence** is a group of words that tells a complete thought. It tells *who* or *what* is doing something, and it tells *what* they are doing.

## ● Making Sure That Sentences Are Clear

The sentences you just looked at were very good, but other sentences are not always clear. Does this next group of words make sense to you?

Beth my friend best is very.

You can see that the words are mixed up. If we put these words in the right order, then we can write a clear sentence.

Beth is my very best friend.

Now look at another group of words. Is it a clear sentence?

do lots of things together.

This is only part of a sentence. In order to make it clear, the writer has to tell *who* does lots of things together.

**My dog and I** do lots of things together.

Look at another example. Is this a sentence?

In the first season we

This group of words doesn't tell us *what happened* in the first season. A good sentence must complete the thought by telling what someone *does* or what something *is*.

In the first season we **won ten games.**

#  Writing for the Reader

When you write a sentence, it is important to remember that someone else is going to read it. These guidelines will help you write sentences that make sense to the reader:

- The words must be in the right *order.*

- It is important to let the reader know *what the sentence is about.* You must tell *who* or *what* is doing something.

- You must tell *what is happening* in the sentence.

When you write sentences this way, the reader can understand what you are saying. You must also remember two other things that help make your sentences clear:

- A **capital letter** is used at the beginning of the first word of *every* sentence. This shows the reader where the sentence begins.

- A **period** (.) is used to show that a *statement* has been completed. This shows the reader where the sentence ends.

  **My** frog hopped onto the teacher's desk.

Later we will see other marks that are used at the end of other kinds of sentences.

# The Subject of the Sentence

Every sentence must contain two important parts. One of these parts is the **subject.** The other is called the predicate.

> • The **subject** tells what the sentence is about. It tells *who* or *what* is doing something.

This is easy to remember because the subject is *the person or thing you are talking about.* In each of the following sentences the **subject** is in dark print.*

> **Mom** helped me with my homework.
>
> **We** watched all the games in the World Series.
>
> **My grandfather** plays beach ball with me.
>
> **The airplane** was flying very low and fast.
>
> **They** are coming to visit some time next week.

In some sentences the subject was a **noun** that told who or what was doing something (*Mom, grandfather, airplane*). Nouns are words that name people, places or things. In other sentences, the subject was a **pronoun** which told us who was doing something (*We, They*). Pronouns are words that take the place of nouns.

You will learn more about nouns and pronouns in Chapter 2 of this book.

---

\* We will often emphasize certain words by printing them in darker letters called **boldface.** Other words will be emphasized in slanted letters called *italics.* Remember that **boldface** and *italics* refer to these two kinds of printing.

# The Predicate of the Sentence

There is another part of the sentence that is just as important as the subject. This part of the sentence is called the **predicate.**

> • The **predicate** tells something about the subject. It tells what the subject *is* or what it is *doing*.

If you read a sentence about astronauts who flew to the moon, the predicate is the part that tells you what the astronauts *did:* they *flew* to the moon. You can find the predicate in a sentence by asking yourself, "What is the subject *doing* or what does this tell me *about* the subject?"

The **predicate** is in boldface in these sentences:

Everybody in class **looks out the window.**

My dog **barks at anybody he doesn't know.**

Nobody **knows what is going on.**

In these sentences, the predicate begins with words that tell what something *is* or what it is *doing: looks, barks, knows.* These words are called **verbs.** The verb is the most important part of the predicate. Many verbs express action: *look, run, jump, play, swim.* Some verbs tell about other things we can do: *know, see, read, write.* Other important verbs are *is, was, are, be, have, has, do, go,* and *come.*

You will find out more about verbs in Chapter 3 of this book. For now, just remember that the verb is the most important part of the predicate. It is the word that tells what the subject *is* or what it *does.*

# Declarative Sentences and Interrogative Sentences

Many sentences make statements.

It was raining very hard this morning.

I dropped my books in a puddle.

The plane flew across the ocean in five hours.

English colonists settled in Virginia in 1607.

These sentences tell us what happened or they give us information. Sentences that make statements are called **declarative sentences.**

> • **Declarative sentences** begin with a capital letter. A period (**.**) is used at the end of each declarative sentence.

Other sentences ask **questions.**

Where is my other sock?

Have you already seen this movie?

Who is going to bring the potato chips?

These are called **interrogative sentences.** The word *interrogate* means "to ask questions."

> • **Interrogative sentences** begin with a capital letter. A question mark (**?**) is used at the end of each interrogative sentence.

# Declarative Sentences and Interrogative Sentences (continued)

Declarative sentences often begin with the **subject.** Then the **predicate** appears later in the sentence. These sentences tell us *who* is doing something and then tell us *what they are doing.* In the following sentences, the subject is printed in **boldface.**

> **He** is going to the movies this afternoon.
>
> **They** were shopping for a new car.
>
> **She** was planning to leave before noon.

Interrogative sentences often begin with part of the **predicate.** Then the **subject** appears later in the sentence. This change in *word order* makes the difference between a statement and a question.

> Is **he** going to the movies this afternoon?
>
> Were **they** shopping for a new car?
>
> Was **she** planning to leave before noon?

Interrogative sentences also may begin with words that signal "THIS IS A QUESTION." Some of these signal words are used in the following interrogative sentences.

> **Why** did you do that?
>
> **Where** is everybody?
>
> **When** will we get there?
>
> **Which** elephant is yours?
>
> **Who** is knocking at the door?
>
> **What** are you looking for?

# Imperative Sentences

Most statements and questions have a **subject** and a **predicate** written out, but here are some sentences that are different. In these sentences the subject is *not* written out.

> Please close the door when you leave.
>
> Write your name on your paper.
>
> Ask someone for directions.

These sentences do not make a statement or ask a question. They give *commands* or make *requests* that ask someone to do something. These are called **imperative sentences.** The word *imperative* means that something needs to be done *right now.*

- **Imperative sentences** begin with a capital letter. A period (**.**) is used at the end of each imperative sentence. In an imperative sentence, the subject is usually understood and is not written out.

In imperative sentences the verb comes right at the beginning or may be preceded by the word *please.* The subject of an imperative sentence is **understood** because the request or command is spoken to the listener.

In the following imperative sentences the subject is shown in parentheses ( ).

> (You)    Look out for the wet paint.
>
> (Lisa)    Please explain that again.
>
> (Ricky)  See if the clothes are dry.

# Exclamatory Sentences

Sometimes you may want to write sentences that make very *strong statements*.

That was a fantastic movie!

I almost jumped out of my skin!

I don't know when I've been so angry !

Sentences that make strong statements are called **exclamatory sentences.** The word *exclaim* means "to cry out suddenly."

- **Exclamatory sentences** are used to show strong feelings such as surprise or anger. Exclamatory sentences begin with a capital letter. An exclamation mark **(!)** is used at the end of each exclamatory sentence.

Look at these pairs of sentences. The first sentence in each pair makes a statement, but the second one says the same thing more strongly. In each pair, the second sentence is an **exclamatory sentence.**

That was hard to believe. I couldn't believe it!

That was a very good game. What a great game that was!

It was a scary movie. I was so scared I almost fainted!

The food was very good. That was the best meal I ever ate!

# The Complete Subject and the Simple Subject

Sometimes the subject of a sentence contains only one or two words. Subjects may be longer, but you can always find the subject by asking, "Who or what is this sentence about?"

In the following examples you see a short line between the subject and the predicate. The words that come before the short line make up the **complete subject** of each sentence.

| COMPLETE SUBJECT | PREDICATE |
|---|---|
| These books | are very heavy. |
| Both football teams | made a lot of mistakes. |
| Two of my friends | took a long trip last summer. |

When a subject contains several words, there is usually one word that tells *exactly* who or what is doing something. This word is called the **simple subject.** In the next examples the simple subject is printed in **boldface.**

**We** | like to play soccer.

The **people** next door | moved away.

Every **person** in the room | stood up.

My whole **family** | likes to go on picnics.

- The **complete subject** includes *all* the words in the subject part of the sentence.
- The **simple subject** tells exactly *who* or *what* the sentence is about.

# The Complete Predicate and the Simple Predicate

In the next examples, the subject of each sentence is the pronoun *I*. The predicate begins with the verb *see* and continues with all the words needed to make the sentence complete. This is called the **complete predicate** of the sentence.

SUBJECT | COMPLETE PREDICATE

I   |   **see** my friend.

I   |   **see** my friend across the street.

I   |   **see** my friend across the street with her mom.

The most important part of the predicate is the **verb** which tells what the subject *does* or what it *is*. This is called the **simple predicate.** In the sentences above, the simple predicate is the verb *see*. In the following sentences, the simple predicate is printed in **boldface.**

My friends | **live** close to me.

We | **have looked** through all these old magazines.

All these kids | **are** my good friends.

My grandparents | **will come** to see us next week.

---

- The **complete predicate** includes *all* the words in the predicate part of the sentence.
- The **simple predicate** is the verb that tells exactly what the subject *is* or what it *does*.

---

## ☑ CHECK YOUR UNDERSTANDING
### ANSWERS BEGIN ON PAGE 219.

## Writing Complete Sentences

*You may want to write the answers on a separate sheet of paper.*

1. Look at the group of words after each number. If it is a clear, complete sentence, then write the word **YES.** If it is not a sentence, then write the word **NO**.

    1. One of my favorite sports is golf.

    2. When we can't ride the horses by ourselves.

    3. They were sitting around watching the news.

    4. because it helps kids to learn.

2. Some of these groups of words are not in the right order. Others do not tell who is doing something or what they are doing. Make the changes needed to write complete sentences. Add your own words when necessary.

    1. When I grow up I a football player.

    2. find them anywhere in my closet.

    3. My family and I to California last year.

    4. watch like TV or play I ball to.

3. Here are some groups of words that aren't complete. Add a word in each blank space to write a good sentence. Here is an example:

    > She _____ a large package.
    > She **carried** a large package.

    1. _____ was surprised to see them.

    2. The students were _____ on the playground.

    3. _____ looked under the bed and in the closet.

    4. He can _____ faster than anybody I know.

➡ *If you have trouble with any of these, talk to your parent or teacher.*

# CHECK YOUR UNDERSTANDING ☑

## The Subject of the Sentence

*You may want to write the answers on a separate sheet of paper.*

1. Draw a short line after the **complete subject** of each sentence. Here is an example:

   Kim's mother | is a doctor.

   1. Sometimes our dog roams all over the neighborhood.

   2. Once a girl named Stacie stayed at a hotel with her parents.

   3. Tony and I wanted to go downtown after school.

   4. Our soccer team is in second place.

   5. My best friend rides the bus with me.

2. After each number, write the **complete subject** of each sentence. Then underline the **simple subject.**

   1. I want to be a swimming teacher.

   2. The people next door are away on vacation.

   3. Many ships sailed along the coast every day.

   4. Three planes were waiting on the runway.

   5. One large truck was painted red and white.

3. Look at each group of words written below. If the group of words is a complete sentence, then underline the **complete subject.** If the group of words does *not* have a subject, then *add a subject.*

   1. The game lasted longer than I thought it would.

   2. wrote a secret message in the book.

   3. is the coldest day in years.

   4. She felt better after the snow stopped.

   5. found the gerbil in the heater pipe.

➡ *If you have trouble with any of these, talk to your parent or teacher.*

**1**

## ☑ CHECK YOUR UNDERSTANDING

### The Predicate of the Sentence

*You may want to write answers on a separate sheet of paper.*

1.  In each of these sentences, a blank space shows where a verb has been left out. Add a **simple predicate** that tells what the subject *did.* Sometimes you can choose one of several words that would make sense. Here is an example:

    > One night I _____ a bright light outside my window.
    > One night I **saw** a bright light outside my window.

    1. Then he _____ outside to get some fresh air.

    2. Julie and I _____ in line for our turn.

    3. In the magic jungle there _____ a unicorn.

    4. The next day he _____ to dig under the wall.

    5. Sometimes she _____ me bowling or skating.

2.  Look at each sentence and decide what the predicate is. Underline the **complete predicate.** Be sure to include all the words that tell about the subject or tell what the subject *did.* Then add another line under the word that is the **simple predicate.**

    1. This fish is much larger than the others.

    2. One day he decided to run away.

    3. My neighbors had an old dog named Ralph.

    4. The scientists analyzed the slimy stuff.

    5. I got a bad sunburn at the beach.

➥ *If you have trouble with any of these, talk to your parent or teacher.*

# CHECK YOUR UNDERSTANDING ☑

## Declarative and Interrogative Sentences

*You may want to write answers on a separate sheet of paper.*

**1.** Some of these sentences make statements and some ask questions. Rewrite each **statement** so that it becomes a **question.** Rewrite each **question** so that it becomes a **statement.** Remember to change the punctuation mark at the end of each sentence. Here is an example:

> They are looking under the house for their frog.
> **Are** they looking under the house for their frog**?**

1. She will go to camp next summer.

2. The game will be played on Monday.

3. Did they hear the thunderstorm last night?

4. They do like to read adventure stories.

5. Will Erica carry these packages into the house?

**2.** These sentences make statements. Use the signal words ***who, what, when, why, how*** to change each statement to a question. If you think of each statement as the **answer,** then you can decide what the **question** should be. Be sure to change the period to a question mark at the end of each question. Here is an example:

> Everybody has gone home.
> **Where** is everybody**?**

1. They will come back tomorrow. (When)

2. He hurt his arm playing football. (How)

3. Mike and Andy were the last ones to leave. (Who)

4. I want to be a superstar when I grow up. (What)

5. The table fell over because the leg broke. (Why)

➡ *If you have trouble with any of these, talk to your parent or teacher.*

☑ *Check Your Understanding*

## Imperative and Exclamatory Sentences

*You may want to write the answers on a separate sheet of paper.*

1. Correct the sentences below. Be sure to add a capital letter at the beginning of each sentence. If the sentence gives a **command,** end it with a *period.* If the sentence makes an **exclamation,** end it with an *exclamation mark.*

    1. that was the most fun I ever had

    2. tell me how you figured that out

    3. what an incredible catch that was

    4. he was the greatest ball player I ever saw

2. Each of these sentences makes a simple statement. Rewrite each sentence so that it becomes an **exclamation.** Here is an example:

    The game lasted a long time. I thought the game would never end!

    1. The rain was falling harder than you can imagine.

    2. It was difficult to believe our eyes.

    3. The wind and snow were blowing very hard.

    4. My shoes can't be found.

3. Each of these sentences asks a question. Rewrite each question so that it becomes a **command.** Notice that each question has *you* as the subject. When you change these questions to commands, the subject *you* will be understood. Here is an example:

    Will you see who is at the door? See who is at the door.

    1. Can you find the answer to this question?

    2. Can you find out how long we have to wait?

    3. Will you tell me how you got that answer?

    4. Can you answer the phone?

➡ *If you have trouble with any of these, talk to your parent or teacher.*

# NOUNS AND PRONOUNS
## Words That Name Things

*In Chapter 1 we looked at sentences to see how they are organized. Now we will look at specific words to find out how they are used within sentences.*

## NOUNS

These sentences were written by students your age. Look at the words printed in **boldface** in each sentence.

> I'm going to **Florida** this **summer**. It's always **fun** when I go there. I swim and ride my **bike** and my **skateboard**. I made some new **friends** when I was there last **year**.

> Last **June** I went to see my **aunt** and **uncle**. They both teach **school** in **Arkansas**. They live near a big **city**, but I can't remember the **name** of it.

Some of these words refer to people: friends, aunt, uncle. Other words refer to places: Florida, Arkansas, school, city. Finally, some of these words refer to things: bike, skateboard. Each of these words is used to *name* something or someone, and each of these words is a **noun**.

> • **Nouns** are words that name people, places, or things.

• THE BASE FORM OF NOUNS

A **base word** is the form of the word that gives its basic meaning. It is the word as it exists without any special endings added. Nouns can be used in their base form, and they can be changed by the addition of word endings.

## ● Singular Nouns and Plural Nouns

Most of the nouns we saw were base words that named only *one* person, place, or thing. These are called **singular nouns**. When we want to name *more than one* thing we use **plural nouns**. *Singular* means "one" and *plural* means "more than one."

Usually a plural noun is formed by adding the letter *s* to the end of the singular noun.

| Singular | Plural | Singular | Plural |
|----------|--------|----------|--------|
| teacher | teachers | group | groups |
| apple | apples | collar | collars |
| building | buildings | position | positions |
| blizzard | blizzards | disease | diseases |

For some nouns we must add *es* instead of *s* to show the plural. Add *es* to nouns that end with these sounds:

the /s/ sound in *bus* or *grass*     the /ks/ sound in *box*

the /sh/ sound in *wish*     the /ch/ sound in *inch* or *watch*

Here are a few nouns that add *es* to form the plural:

| Singular | Plural | Singular | Plural |
|----------|--------|----------|--------|
| bus | buses | dish | dishes |
| class | classes | bunch | bunches |
| fox | foxes | patch | patches |

## ● Special Endings for Some Plural Nouns

Some singular nouns end with a **consonant** followed by the letter **y**. To write the plural form of these nouns, **change the final y to i and add es.**

| | |
|---|---|
| sky, sk**ies** | baby, bab**ies** |
| city, cit**ies** | penny, penn**ies** |
| story, stor**ies** | famil**y**, famil**ies** |

When a noun ends with a **vowel** followed by the letter **y**, **add only the letter s to form the plural.**

| | |
|---|---|
| boy, boys | toy, toys |
| day, days | highway, highways |
| monkey, monkeys | chimney, chimneys |
| pie, pies | movie, movies |

It is important to look at the letters at the end of a singular noun before you add **s** or **es** to form the plural. The combination of **vowels** and **consonants** at the end of the singular noun will tell you which ending to use. Remember that **vowels** are the letters **a, e, i, o, u.** The letter **y** can also be a vowel, especially in words such as *baby* and *city*. All the other letters are **consonants**.

## ● Irregular Plural Nouns

Some nouns do not add **s** or **es** to form the plural. These nouns **change the vowel sound** in the middle of the word. There are only a few of these nouns, and you probably already know them. Here are some **irregular plural nouns** that you often use:

| | |
|---|---|
| foot, feet | tooth, teeth |
| man, men | woman, women |
| child, children | person, people |
| mouse, mice | goose, geese |

# ● Common Nouns and Proper Nouns

**Common nouns** name *any* person, place, or thing.

Some **children** were on the playground.

We went to a big **hospital** to visit my friend.

Some of these **books** are very interesting to read.

These common nouns do not say exactly *which* children or *which* hospital or *which* books are being described.

**Proper nouns** name *specific* people or places or things. *Proper nouns are always capitalized.*

**Bill** and **Ellen** are doing their homework.

We visited **Chicago** and **Milwaukee**.

The **Grand Canyon** is in **Arizona**.

The proper nouns in these sentences tell exactly *who* is doing their homework, and they tell exactly *which cities* were visited. The proper nouns in the last sentence name a specific canyon in a specific state.

Your name is a proper noun, and the names of all your friends and your relatives and your teachers are also proper nouns. The name of each city and state and country is a proper noun. The names of the months and days of the week are also proper nouns.

COMMON NOUNS name any
**person:** president
**place:** city
**thing:** monument

PROPER NOUNS name a specific
**person:** Abraham Lincoln
**place:** Washington, D.C.
**thing:** Lincoln Memorial

## • MORE ABOUT COMMON NOUNS & PROPER NOUNS

Some proper nouns contain several words. When this happens, only the *most important* words are capitalized. You do not need to capitalize short words such as *of, to, at,* or *in.*

**Maria Lopez** and **Ellen Brown** visited our class.

**North Dakota** is next to **Minnesota**.

The **Declaration of Independence** was signed in 1776.

Her full name is **Mary Elizabeth Green**.

The **Statue of Liberty** is in **New York**.

**Canada** is north of the **United States of America**.

Some **common nouns** are listed below on the left. The list on the right gives some **proper nouns** that are examples of the people or places or things shown in the list of common nouns. You can see that *Boston* is a specific *city, France* is a specific *country, Monday* is a specific *day,* etc .

| Common Noun | Proper Nouns |
|---|---|
| city | Boston, Dallas, Los Angeles |
| country | France, United States of America |
| state | Nevada, Pennsylvania, West Virginia |
| president | George Washington, Thomas Jefferson |
| ocean | Atlantic Ocean, Pacific Ocean |
| day | Monday, Tuesday, Wednesday |
| month | January, February, March |
| river | Mississippi River, Ohio River |
| holiday | Christmas, New Year's Day, Fourth of July |

In the next two sentences you can see the difference between common nouns and proper nouns. The second sentence uses **proper nouns** to show exactly who the first sentence is talking about and where they went.

Two of my **friends** visited a big **city** on vacation.

**Susan** and **Kim** visited **New York** on vacation.

**2** ELEMENTARY GRAMMAR

## ● Singular Possessive Nouns

These sentences tell that someone *owns* a certain thing.

This book belongs to Jan.

That coat belongs to Robert.

There is still another way to show ownership: a **possessive noun** can be used to indicate that something belongs to someone. The following sentences show **singular possessive nouns** written in boldface.

This is **Jan's** book.     That is **Robert's** coat.

> • A **singular possessive noun** shows that something belongs to *one* person, place, or thing. To write a singular possessive noun, add an **apostrophe** and the letter *s ('s)* after a singular noun.

Here are sentences which first tell you that something belongs to someone or to something. Then each sentence is written again using a **singular possessive noun** to show the same thing.

This bike belongs to Mary. It is **Mary's** bike.

That umbrella belongs to Mom. It is **Mom's** umbrella.

This collar belongs to my dog. It is my **dog's** collar.

This flag belongs to my country. It is my **country's** flag.

In these sentences you have seen the ***apostrophe*** and *s* (***'s***) added to singular nouns to show that something belongs to *one* person or *one* thing. The spelling of the noun does not change at all.

# ⬤ Plural Possessive Nouns

You know that many plural nouns end with *s* or *es*. The following sentences use **plural possessive nouns** to show that something belongs to several people or places or things.

> We're trying to find parking places for these two cars.
>     Where are the **cars'** parking places?

> I can't find the batteries for these three watches.
>     Have you seen the **watches'** new batteries?

> Two of my friends are going to spend the day with me.
>     My **friends'** names are Frank and Jaime.

> Four of the small towns got new fire trucks.
>     The **towns'** fire trucks just arrived.

---

- **A plural possessive noun** shows that something belongs to *more than one* person, place, or thing. To write a plural possessive noun, add only an **apostrophe** *(')* after plural nouns ending with *s* or *es.*

---

Here are some more sentences which tell about things that belong to several people or things. The second sentence in each pair uses **plural possessive nouns** that add an apostrophe after the final letters *s* or *es.*

> These books belong to Nancy and Sue. These are the **girls'** books.

> Those bikes belong to Bill and Ed and Walter. They are the **boys'** bikes.

> These bushes have many thorns. Watch out for these **bushes'** thorns.

> I can't find the packing boxes for these dishes. Where are the **dishes'** boxes?

• POSSESSIVE NOUNS ENDING WITH *Y, EY,* AND *IE*

Nouns that end with a consonant and **y** change the final **y** to **i** before adding **es** to form the plural. When you want to use these words as **possessive nouns,** add **'s** in the singular form. For the plural, add only an **apostrophe** after the **ies** ending.

|  |  |
|---|---|
| baby's, babies' | puppy's, puppies' |
| city's, cities' | pony's, ponies' |

Words that end with **ey** add **'s** in the singular to show possession. The plural form already ends with the letter **s,** so you add only an **apostrophe** after the final **s.**

|  |  |
|---|---|
| key's, keys' | monkey's, monkeys' |
| valley's, valleys' | turkey's, turkeys' |

Nouns that end with **ie** also add **'s** in the singular to show possession. The plural form already ends with **s,** so you add *only* the **apostrophe** after the final **s.**

|  |  |
|---|---|
| pie's, pies' | tie's, ties' |
| movie's, movies' | prairie's, prairies' |

## Irregular Plural Possessive Nouns

On page 19 you saw some **irregular plural nouns** that do *not* add **s** or **es** to form the plural. For these words, add **'s** to show possession in the singular *or* the plural.

Here is one **woman's** hat. There are two **women's** hats.

This is the **man's** coat. These are the **men's** coats.

Here is one **child's** book. There are two **children's** books.

This is one **person's** car. These are three **people's** cars.

# PRONOUNS

Look at these sentences:

**Maria** is very good in math. **Maria** knows a lot about computers, and **Maria** wants to be a scientist when **Maria** grows up.

We certainly can tell that these sentences are talking about *Maria*. Every sentence begins with her name. However, we really don't need to repeat Maria's name so many times. Look at the words printed in **boldface** in the following sentences:

**Maria** is very good in math. **She** knows a lot about computers, and **she** wants to be a scientist when **she** grows up.

Maria's name is used only once. Even so, we still know that all the sentences are talking about *Maria*. Instead of repeating her name, we have used the word *she* in several places.

The word *she* is a **pronoun**. It was used to take the place of Maria's name, and it helps us know that the sentences are all talking about her.

> • A **pronoun** is a word that takes the place of a noun or nouns.

**Pronouns** help us write sentences without constantly repeating the name of the person or the thing we are talking about. Here are a few more sentences that use pronouns:

**I** am going to tell **you** about a problem **we** had.

**We** wanted to leave, but **they** weren't ready.

John said that **he** lost his watch, but **he** found **it** later.

# Subject Pronouns and Object Pronouns

- THE PRONOUNS *I, ME,* AND *YOU*

The pronoun *I* is used to take the place of *your name* in the subject part of the sentence. *This word is always capitalized,* even when it is not the first word in the sentence. The word *I* is a **subject pronoun** which shows that you are the person who is doing something.

> I ran into the house when the rain started.
>
> I did my homework before dinner for a change.

In the **predicate** of the sentence, the pronoun *me* is used when you are talking about yourself.

> Mom gave the books to **me.**
>
> Dad thanked **me** for mowing the lawn.

The word *me* is an **object pronoun**. It is used after the verb in the predicate part of the sentence when you are talking about yourself.

- USING *I* AND *ME* WITH OTHER PEOPLE'S NAMES

When you talk about yourself *and* other people, always give their names first. After their names, use *I* in the subject part of the sentence and use *me* in the predicate.

> Erica and Joan and I are friends.
> (**NOT**  I and Erica and Joan are friends.)
>
> The teacher asked Bill and **me** some questions.
> (**NOT**  The teacher asked me and Bill some questions.)

## ● More Subject and Object Pronouns

- THE PRONOUNS *WE* AND *US*

What pronouns do you use when you are talking about yourself *and* other people? Would you always have to use the names of the other people in every sentence?

> Bill and Evan and I play basketball a lot. Bill and Evan and I are not very good yet, but Bill and Evan and I are getting better.

Instead of repeating all these names, you can use the pronoun *we* to refer to yourself and other people. The word *we* is a **subject pronoun**.

> Bill and Evan and I play basketball a lot. **We** are not very good yet, but **we** are getting better.

In the **predicate** part of the sentence, the pronoun *us* is used when you are talking about yourself and other people. *Us* is an **object pronoun**. You can see how *us* is used in the following sentences. The second sentence of each pair uses *us* to take the place of the names given in the first sentence.

> Dad gave the books to Kim and me.
> Dad gave the books to **us.**
>
> Mom called my brother and me.
> Mom called **us.**

These sentences were written by students your age. They show how the pronouns *we* and *us* are used.

> **We** were playing on the sliding board.
>
> My mom and dad took **us** to see the movie.
>
> **We** go to Girl Scouts together.
>
> Our teacher showed **us** some eggs.
>
> Soon **we** will be out of school.

## More Subject and Object Pronouns

• THE PRONOUNS *HE, SHE,* AND *IT*

We often talk about *another* person, place, or thing, not about ourselves. To do this, we can use the singular pronouns *he, she*, and *it*. These are **subject pronouns**.

> Ray is a good student. **He** also plays football.
>
> Sally likes to ski. **She** is a good skater, too.
>
> Chicago is a big city. **It** is on Lake Michigan.
>
> This coat doesn't fit. **It** is much too large.

In the **predicate** part of the sentence, we must use different forms of the pronoun to refer to another person. Look at each of these pairs of sentences. In the first sentence of each pair, a pronoun is used as the subject. In the second sentence of each pair, a different form of that pronoun is used in the predicate.

> **She** likes to read. I gave **her** some books.
>
> **He** is in my school. I saw **him** yesterday.

The words *her* and *him* are **object pronouns**. They are used after the verb that tells what happens in the sentence.

The singular pronoun *it* is used to refer to a place or a thing. This pronoun is the same in the subject and the predicate.

> This is my bike. **It** is new. I like to ride **it**.
>
> Cleveland is in Ohio. **It** is on Lake Erie. I visited **it**.

# More Subject and Object Pronouns

- ## THE PRONOUNS *HIM* AND *HER*

When we want to use pronouns in the **predicate** part of the sentence to talk about another person, we use the **object pronouns** *him* and *her*. These sentences show how to use *he* and *him, she* and *her:*

> **He** is playing ball. (**He** is the subject pronoun.)
> This package is for **him**. (**Him** is the object pronoun.)
> I couldn't see **him** anywhere. (**Him** is the object pronoun.)
>
> **She** was looking for her book. (**She** is the subject pronoun.)
> I gave the books to **her**. (**Her** is the object pronoun.)
> We found **her** in the park. (**Her** is the object pronoun.)

- ## THE PRONOUNS *THEY* AND *THEM*

We use the plural pronoun *they* to refer to other people or places or things, not to ourselves. The word *they* is a **subject pronoun**.

> Bill, Kate, and Dan were not in school. **They** stayed home.

> These two books are very good. **They** are fun to read.

In the predicate of the sentence we use the plural pronoun *them* to talk about several other people or things. The word *them* is an **object pronoun**.

> I gave my pencils to **them**. (The word **them** tells who received your pencils.)

> We saw **them** at school yesterday. (The word **them** tells who was seen at school yesterday.)

## Showing the Relationship between Nouns and Pronouns

Whenever you use pronouns, you must be sure that the reader can tell *which* noun or nouns the pronoun replaces. See if the use of the pronoun *he* is clear in this example:

> Juan and Thomas both made the baseball team. **He** is one of the best players in school.

The first sentence contained two subjects: Juan *and* Thomas. The singular pronoun *he* in the second sentence could refer to either name. We can't tell which it should be.

If we really want to refer to only one name, then the second sentence would have to repeat that name in order to make the meaning clear.

> Juan and Thomas both made the baseball team. **Juan** is one of the best players in school.

On the other hand, we might want to say that *both* boys are very good baseball players. Here are the changes we could make if this is what we wanted to say:

> Juan and Thomas both made the baseball team. **They** are the best players in school.

Now the plural pronoun *they* refers to Juan *and* Thomas. We also changed to the plural verb *are* and removed the word *one* because we are talking about both players.

Are the next sentences clear?

> Joan and Sue looked for shoes. **She** found some **she** liked.

We can't tell whether *she* refers to Joan or Ellen. The second sentence can be corrected by making one of these changes:

> Joan and Sue looked for shoes. Joan found some **she** liked.

> Joan and Sue looked for shoes. Sue found some **she** liked.

## Showing the Relationship between Nouns and Pronouns (continued)

In the following sentences, can you tell which noun is being replaced by the pronouns in **boldface?**

Emily told Bob that **he** got the best grade.

Emily told Bob that **they** got the best grades.

These two sentences say different things, and both of them are correct. In the first sentence, the singular pronoun *he* shows that Bob got the best grade. In the second sentence, the plural pronoun *they* shows that *both* Bob and Emily got the best grades.

Ellen got a new coat, and **she** likes **it** very much.

The pronoun *she* refers to Ellen, and the pronoun *it* refers to her coat. Here the pronouns are clear because they match the nouns in the first part of the sentence. Are the next sentences just as clear?

The student waited an hour for the bus. **They** thought it would never arrive.

The subject of the first sentence is *student,* which is singular. The pronoun *they* in the second sentence is plural and cannot be used to take the place of a singular noun. The pronoun *he* or *she* should be used in the second sentence.

- Whenever you use pronouns, be sure that they agree in *number* with the nouns they replace. Singular pronouns must take the place of singular nouns, and plural pronouns must take the place of plural nouns.
- Use **subject pronouns** in the subject of the sentence and **object pronouns** in the predicate of the sentence.

# Possessive Pronouns

We have seen **subject pronouns** and **object pronouns** used to take the place of **nouns**. We can also use **possessive pronouns** to take the place of **possessive nouns**.

When we use possessive pronouns, we do *not* add **'s** or any other ending. Instead, we use special forms of pronouns that show ownership. Here are the possessive pronouns in the singular and the plural:

| POSSESSIVE PRONOUNS | | |
|---|---|---|
| | **Singular** | **Plural** |
| 1. | my | our |
| 2. | your | your |
| 3. | his | their |
| | her | |
| | its | |

In the following sentences you will see possessive pronouns in boldface. Each sentence has a subject pronoun near the beginning. The possessive pronoun is used later in the sentence.

I can't find **my** homework papers.

Have you written to **your** grandparents lately?

He said that **his** bicycle was broken.

She knows that **her** parents will be home soon.

We must get **our** tickets before they are sold out.

They are pleased with **their** new house.

## ● Review of Pronouns

The following lists contain all the pronouns we have looked at so far. You can see which pronouns are singular and which are plural. You can also see which pronouns are used as subjects, which are used as objects, and which are used to show possession.

### SUBJECT PRONOUNS

| | Singular | Plural |
|---|---|---|
| 1. | I | we |
| 2. | you | you |
| 3. | he | they |
| | she | |
| | it | |

### OBJECT PRONOUNS

| | Singular | Plural |
|---|---|---|
| 1. | me | us |
| 2. | you | you |
| 3. | him | them |
| | her | |
| | it | |

### POSSESSIVE PRONOUNS

| | Singular | Plural |
|---|---|---|
| 1. | my | our |
| 2. | your | your |
| 3. | his | their |
| | her | |
| | its | |

**2**

## ✓ CHECK YOUR UNDERSTANDING
### ANSWERS BEGIN ON PAGE 224.

## Using Nouns
*You may want to write the answers on a separate sheet of paper.*

1. Use one of these nouns at each place marked by a blank line.

   carpenter    photograph    dentist    medicine    science

   1. This ____ is fuzzy and blurred.

   2. ____ is the study of things in nature.

   3. The ____ is making new cabinets and shelves.

   4. I have an appointment to go to the ____ tomorrow.

   5. The new ____ helped get rid of my cough.

2. A noun is printed in **boldface** in each of the following sentences. Choose some *other* noun that would fit. Here is an example:

   > That **story** was interesting. That **movie** was interesting.

   1. My **hamster** is a very good pet.

   2. Does your **brother** like to eat broccoli?

   3. I can't believe you actually like **snakes**!

   4. They got lost on the way to the **library**.

   5. Is this your **slipper** under the bed?

3. Each of these sentences contains two or three nouns. Write each noun and indicate whether it names a person, a place, or a thing.

   1. This sandwich tastes like cardboard!

   2. His brother and her uncle are good friends.

   3. The carriage traveled from the small town to the city.

   4. Is that a crocodile or an alligator?

   5. The detective and his assistant solved the mystery.

➡ *If you have trouble with any of these, talk to your parent or teacher.*

# CHECK YOUR UNDERSTANDING

## Singular and Plural Nouns

*You may want to write the answers on a separate sheet of paper.*

**1.** Write all the nouns you find in each of these sentences. Indicate whether each noun is **singular** or **plural**. Here is an example:

> Are my books on the table or on the chair?
> *books* (plural)  *table* (singular)  *chair* (singular)

    1. The wheels on all these bicycles are bent.

    2. My cousin and his friends drove across the country.

    3. This sweater is big enough to fit an elephant!

    4. Chipmunks and squirrels ran through the forest.

**2.** Write the following sentences on your paper. Use the **plural** form of one of these nouns in each blank space.

      story     flashlight     closet     turkey     hamburger

    1. That is the noisiest bunch of ____ I ever heard!

    2. Does this house have many ____?

    3. Some of these ____ are not well cooked.

    4. Both ____ need new batteries.

    5. Have you read all the ____ in this book?

**3.** Some of these nouns are singular and some are plural. Write the plural form for each singular noun that you find in the list, and write the singular form for each plural noun. For example, if you saw **babies** on the list, you would write **baby** on your paper.

    1. sentence      4. customers      7. copy

    2. mystery      5. prairie      8. audiences

    3. chimney      6. shoulders      9. fireman

➥ *If you have trouble with any of these, talk to your parent or teacher.*

**2**

# ☑ CHECK YOUR UNDERSTANDING

## Common and Proper Nouns

*You may want to write the answers on a separate sheet of paper.*

1. At the end of each sentence, add a **proper noun** that completes the statement. Remember to capitalize all important words in each proper noun.

   1. My best friend is _____.

   2. A place I would like to visit is _____.

   3. The hottest month in summer is _____.

   4. The busiest street in town is _____.

   5. I live in the state of _____.

2. Add the necessary capital letters to show that each of these is a **proper noun**.

   1. mississippi river       6. japan

   2. saturday                7. november

   3. england                 8. mark twain

   4. main street             9. denver

   5. arizona                 10. united states of america

3. Add any capital letters that may be needed and add a period or question mark at the end of each sentence. Remember to capitalize the first word in the sentence and any proper nouns.

   1. the states of alaska and texas are very large

   2. my friends went to washington and new york at christmas

   3. have you ever seen yellowstone park or the grand canyon

   4. we flew across the pacific ocean to hawaii

   5. are germany and spain both in europe

➥ *If you have trouble with any of these, talk to your parent or teacher.*

# CHECK YOUR UNDERSTANDING

## Possessive Nouns

*You may want to write the answers on a separate sheet of paper.*

1. Add the **apostrophe (' )** in the correct place to show that these are **singular possessive nouns.**

    1. I finally found my **dogs** collar.

    2. Where is your **cousins** house?

    3. The game is at my **sisters** school.

    4. Is this your **friends** bicycle?

    5. **Franks** parents came to the meeting.

2. Add **'s** to form a **singular possessive noun** for each word in boldface.

    1. The **lion** roar scared everybody at the zoo.

    2. I found my **brother** shoe under the chair.

    3. Is **Mike** bicycle still out in the rain?

    4. This is the **girl** camera.

    5. When did **Kim** sister arrive in town?

3. These sentences all contain **plural possessive nouns.** When you write them on your paper, be sure to add the **apostrophe (')** where it is needed.

    1. All of my **neighbors** yards are full of leaves.

    2. The **childrens** parents are visiting their school.

    3. Are those the **players** caps and uniforms?

    4. All of my **sisters** friends came to visit at the same time.

    5. The **womens** coats are piled on my bed.

➡ *If you have trouble with any of these, talk to your parent or teacher.*

**2**

## ☑ CHECK YOUR UNDERSTANDING

### The Pronouns *I, me, you, we, us*

*You may want to write the answers on a separate sheet of paper.*

**1.** Each of these sentences contains mistakes in the use of pronouns. **Rewrite the sentences and make the needed corrections.**

    1. Me and John are good friends.

    2. They gave gifts to my sister and I.

    3. May Alice and me go out to play?

    4. My brother and me went to the movie together.

    5. They were looking for Ted and Evan and I.

**2.** Add the pronoun *I* in the subject part of the sentence. Add *me* in the predicate part of the sentence.

    1. My little brother followed ____ on his skateboard.

    2. My dog and ____ do lots of things together.

    3. Mom asked ____ to clean up my room.

    4. ____ finished my work before the bell rang.

    5. Lisa and ____ have been friends since last year.

**3.** In the blank spaces, use the pronouns *we* and *us* to write about yourself and your friends.

    1. Tom and I are friends, and ____ spend a lot of time together.

    2. ____ ride our bikes and play ball almost every day.

    3. Our parents gave ____ new baseballs and bats.

    4. When ____ play together, ____ argue a lot.

    5. Nothing will keep ____ from being good friends.

➡ *If you have trouble with any of these, talk to your parent or teacher.*

# CHECK YOUR UNDERSTANDING

## The Pronouns *he, she, it, him, her, them, they*

*You may want to write the answers on a separate sheet of paper.*

1.  When you write these sentences on your paper, use *he, she,* or *it* in place of the words written in **boldface.**

    1. **Larry** will be back soon.

    2. **This bike** has two flat tires.

    3. **Margarita** is on the playground now.

    4. **My desk** is falling apart.

    5. **Erica** looked for colored leaves in the fall.

2.  Use *him* or *her* or *it* in place of the words that are printed in **boldface.**

    1. I made a phone call to **Russell**.

    2. Please put **this vase** on the table

    3. Can you meet **Lisa** this afternoon?

    4. I gave **Ed** a piece of birthday cake.

    5. Have you looked everywhere for **your book**?

3.  Use the subject pronoun *they* in place of the nouns that are used as subjects. Use the object pronoun *them* in place of the nouns that are used as objects in the predicate part of the sentence.

    1. **All the students** are taking the test now.

    2. I saw **both of my cousins** at the store yesterday.

    3. **Three of the kittens** were playing on the couch.

    4. When will **Tom and his brother** finish shoveling the snow?

    5. I will ask **Ellen and her mom** when they want to leave.

➥ *If you have trouble with any of these, talk to your parent or teacher.*

**2**

# ☑ CHECK YOUR UNDERSTANDING

## Possessive Pronouns

*You may want to write answers on a separate sheet of paper.*

1. Underline the **possessive pronoun** in each sentence.

    1. Which story is your favorite?

    2. All of his balloons have exploded.

    3. Did you see my green umbrella anywhere?

    4. I can't believe her hair is so long.

    5. Their shoes got awfully muddy.

2. Use a **possessive pronoun** in each blank space. Be sure to see what the **subject** of each sentence is in order to decide which possessive pronoun to use. Here is an example:

    > He is still looking for ___ keys.
    > He is still looking for **his** keys.

    1. Have you finished ___ lunch yet?

    2. They don't seem to know where ___ luggage is.

    3. This toy car doesn't have all ___ wheels.

    4. She is trying to find ___ pencil and paper.

    5. How much did they pay for ___ new car?

➡ *If you have trouble with any of these, talk to your parent or teacher.*

40

# VERBS
## Words That Tell What Happens

Look at the words written in **boldface** in each of these sentences:

My brother | **loves** his new snowshoes.

Mom | **drives** me to school when it is raining.

My sister | **is** in the sixth grade.

Our new neighbors | **have** fourteen cats and a dog.

My grandparents | **visit** us every summer.

All my friends | **gave** me a surprise party.

Each of the boldface words is a **verb**. Each verb comes right after the short line that separates the complete subject from the complete predicate.

- The **verb** is the main word in the predicate of every sentence. Verbs tell what the subject of the sentence *is* or what it *does*. Many verbs express *actions*.

## Action Verbs

Action verbs tell what the subject of the sentence is *doing.* Verbs such as *run, jump, throw,* and *hit* express very strong actions. Other verbs such as *talk, look, read,* and *write* also tell about things we *do.* All these words are **action verbs.**

In each of these sentences you see an action verb written in boldface:

> My father **loads** ships on the pier.
>
> My brother and I **fight** a lot.
>
> My aunt **teaches** people how to help themselves.
>
> Sometimes I **dream** about what I will do.
>
> My sister **sings** songs to her pet elephant.

### • THE BASE FORM OF VERBS

A **base word** is the form of a word as it is spelled without any special endings added. Now we will look at **verbs** in their base forms. Later we will look at ways that verbs can be changed by adding endings to the base form.

These sentences use action verbs in their base form:

> I **play** with my kangaroo whenever I can.
>
> Jan and I **walk** to school when the weather is good.
>
> My friends **know** a lot of funny stories.

- REGULAR VERBS

The verbs we will look at on the next few pages are **regular verbs**. This means that they follow the same basic pattern when endings are added. Later we will see some *irregular verbs* that do not always follow these patterns.

- VERB TENSES

Verbs can tell that someone is doing something, but they must also tell *when* the action takes place. Some things may be happening right now, but other things may happen at other times.

> - The **tense** of a verb lets the reader know *when* the action of the verb takes place.
> - The *tense* or *time* of the action is shown by adding special endings to the verb or by combining verbs.
> - The three main verb tenses are the **present tense**, the **past tense**, and the **future tense**.

| | |
|---|---|
| **Present:** | I **work** in the yard when the weather is good. |
| **Past:** | I **worked** on the bushes last Saturday. |
| **Future:** | I **will work** on the grass next Saturday. |

# Regular Verbs in the Present Tense

- Verbs in the **present tense** tell about things that happen right now or things that happen over and over again.

In these sentences each verb is in the **present tense:**

My brother and I **fight** a lot.

His dog **eats** everything he can find.

Sometimes I **dream** about what I will do.

In the present tense we often use verbs in their *base form.* However, it is important to know that a special ending must be added to verbs when they are used with certain subjects.

- ADDING *S* TO THE END OF SOME VERBS

Here you see how the verb *look* is written in the present tense. Notice where the special ending **s** is needed.

**PRESENT TENSE**

|  | Singular | Plural |
|---|---|---|
| 1. | I look | we look |
| 2. | you look | you look |
| 3. | he look**s** | they look |
|  | she look**s** |  |
|  | it look**s** |  |

- In the present tense, add **s** to the end of most regular verbs when the subject is the pronoun *he, she,* or *it.* Also add **s** to the verb when the subject is a **singular noun.**

# Regular Verbs in the Present Tense
(continued)

• ADDING *ES* TO THE END OF SOME VERBS

Some verbs must add *es* instead of *s* after a singular noun or after the pronouns *he, she,* or *it.*

> • In the present tense, add *es* to regular verbs that end with the /s/, /sh/, /ch/, or /ks/ sounds.

Here are some examples of verbs that add *es* when the subject is a singular noun or the pronouns *he, she,* or *it:*

The /s/ sound in **miss:** He **misses** his friends.

The /sh/ sound in **wash:** She **washes** the car on Saturdays.

The /ch/ sound in **catch:** He **catches** for our team.

The /z/ sound in **buzz:** The fly **buzzes** around our heads.

The /ks/ sound in **mix:** Mom **mixes** the egg and flour.

These sentences use verbs that add *es* after the final consonants *ss, sh, ch, z,* or *x:*

My cat **whizzes** up and down the stairs.

Paul's pet parakeet **pushes** peanuts with his beak.

He always **guesses** when he doesn't know the answer.

My pet hamster **watches** cartoons on TV.

Dad always **waxes** the car just before each rainstorm.

**3**

# Regular Verbs in the Present Tense
(continued)

• ADDING *ES* TO VERBS THAT END WITH *Y*

When we looked at *nouns* ending with **y,** we saw that the final **y** changed to **i** before **es** was added. The same thing happens in the present tense when we add **es** to *verbs* that end with **y.**

> • In the present tense, verbs that end with the letter **y** change the **y** to **i** before adding **es.** The **es** ending for the verb is used with singular nouns and with the pronouns *he, she,* or *it.*

Here you see the verb *hurry* in the singular and the plural:

**PRESENT TENSE**

| | Singular | Plural |
|---|---|---|
| 1. | I hurry | we hurry |
| 2. | you hurry | you hurry |
| 3. | he hurr**ies** | they hurry |
| | she hurr**ies** | |
| | it hurr**ies** | |

These sentences use verbs that change **y** to **i** before the ending **es** is added:

This truck **carries** more than both of those smaller ones.

My brother always **cries** when his spinach is overcooked.

That huge sofa **occupies** too much space in this room.

He **worries** too much.

This new cloth **dries** very quickly.

# Regular Verbs in the Present Tense
(continued)

- AGREEMENT OF SUBJECTS AND VERBS

It is important for the subject and the verb of every sentence to *agree*. This means that a *singular* verb must be used with a *singular* subject, and a *plural* verb must be used with a *plural* subject.

---

- In the present tense, use the verb in its **base form** when the subject is *I, you,* or any plural noun or pronoun. No special verb ending is required.
- Add *s* or *es* to the verb in order to make it agree when the subject is a **singular noun** or the pronouns *he, she,* or *it.*

---

Look at the sentences below. The verbs do not agree with their subjects in the first sentence of each example. The second sentence corrects the mistake.

Fred and Ernest plays football better than I do.
Fred and Ernest **play** football better than I do.
  (The verb **play** agrees with the plural subject *Fred and Ernest.)*

One of my shoes are muddy and scuffed.
One of my shoes **is** muddy and scuffed.
  (The verb **is** agrees with the singular subject *one.* The word *shoes* is not the subject and does not affect the verb.)

The dinosaur bones in the museum is really enormous.
The dinosaur bones in the museum **are** really enormous.
  (The verb **are** agrees with the plural subject *bones.* The word *museum* is not the subject and does not affect the verb.)

47

# Regular Verbs in the Past Tense

We just looked at verbs which tell about things that are happening in the present or things that happen over and over again. When we want to tell about things that happened in the past, we use verbs in the **past tense**.

- Verbs in the **past tense** tell about things that have already happened. Many verbs show the past tense by adding *ed* to the end of the base form of the verb.

When verbs add *ed* to show the past tense, they use the same ending in all forms of the singular and the plural. Here are the spellings for the past tense of the verb *walk:*

**PAST TENSE**

| | Singular | Plural |
|---|---|---|
| 1. | I walked | we walked |
| 2. | you walked | you walked |
| 3. | he walked | they walked |
| | she walked | |
| | it walked | |

In the next examples, the first sentence in each pair uses a verb in the **present tense**. The second sentence uses the same verb in the **past tense.**

Today I **learn** about verbs. Last week I **learned** about nouns and pronouns.

She **hopes** to begin her new book soon. Yesterday she **hoped** to finish another book.

They **work** in the yard now. Last Saturday they **worked** in the garage.

# Regular Verbs in the Past Tense
(continued)

- ADDING *ED* TO VERBS THAT END WITH *E*

Some verbs end with the letter *e: use, hope,* and *smile,* for example. With these verbs, just drop the final *e* and add *ed* to form the past tense. Here are some of these verbs written in the **present tense** and then in the **past tense**:

| PRESENT | PAST | PRESENT | PAST |
|---------|------|---------|------|
| use | used | live | lived |
| hope | hoped | bake | baked |
| name | named | care | cared |
| smile | smiled | dance | danced |
| change | changed | scare | scared |

- DOUBLING THE FINAL CONSONANT BEFORE ADDING *ED*

One group of verbs must be written carefully when we add *ed* in the past tense. These are verbs such as *stop* and *drag* that end with a vowel and a consonant as the last two letters.

---

- When a verb ends with a **single vowel** followed by a **single consonant**, the final consonant must be doubled before *ed* is added to form the past tense.

---

# Regular Verbs in the Past Tense
(continued)

The following list shows some verbs that end with this **vowel-consonant pattern**. Notice the spelling of the past tense.

| PRESENT | PAST |
|---------|------|
| hop | ho**pped** |
| skip | ski**pped** |
| stop | sto**pped** |
| drag | dra**gged** |
| slip | sli**pped** |

• CHANGING *Y* TO *I* BEFORE ADDING *ED*

When we looked at verbs in the present tense, we saw that words ending with **y** changed this vowel to **i** before adding **es**. The final **y** must also change to **i** when **ed** is added to form the past tense.

> I usually **study** my lessons after dinner. Yesterday I **studied** for my math test.

> She often **hurries** home after school. Last Friday she **hurried** even faster because it was cold.

Here is how the verb *carry* is written in the past tense. The same spelling is used for the singular *and* the plural.

**PAST TENSE**

| | Singular | Plural |
|---|----------|--------|
| 1. | I carr**ied** | we carr**ied** |
| 2. | you carr**ied** | you carr**ied** |
| 3. | he carr**ied** | they carr**ied** |
| | she carr**ied** | |
| | it carr**ied** | |

- THE REGULAR PATTERN FOR VERBS IN THE PAST TENSE

All the verbs we have seen followed the same pattern in the past tense. *This is the regular pattern* that is used to form the past tense of most verbs.

- **Regular verbs** add *ed* to form the past tense.

Later you will see some irregular verbs that do not always follow this pattern.

# Regular Verbs in the Future Tense

The future tense is used to tell about things that will happen tomorrow or next week or at some time yet to come.

> - The **future tense** combines the verb *will* with the base form of another verb.

Here is the verb *work* written in the future tense.

**FUTURE TENSE**

| | Singular | Plural |
|---|---|---|
| 1. | I will work | we will work |
| 2. | you will work | you will work |
| 3. | he will work | they will work |
| | she will work | |
| | it will work | |

In this example, the word *work* is called the **main verb**, and the word *will* is called the **helping verb.** You will learn more about main verbs and helping verbs on the next page.

In the future tense, the same spelling pattern for the verb is used with every subject, singular and plural. The helping verb *will* is always followed by the base form of the main verb. This is the only pattern used in the future tense.

# ● Main Verbs and Helping Verbs

In Chapter 1 we talked about the **simple predicate** of the sentence. This simple predicate is the *verb* of the sentence. Now you see that the verb may contain more than one word. Many simple predicates contain a **main verb** combined with **helping verbs**.

---

- The **main verb** tells exactly what the subject is or what it is doing.
- **Helping verbs** come just before the main verb. They help the main verb tell exactly *when* something happened.

---

The words *am, are,* and *is* can be used as helping verbs. They are always followed by main verbs that end with **ing.** You use this pattern very often to tell about things that *are happening* at the time you speak or write.

> I **am looking** through these books for a picture of a cow.

> Mom and Dad **are planning** for the party.

> My sister **is practicing** the piano now.

The helping verbs *was* and *were* are also used with main verbs that end with **ing**. This pattern is used to tell about things that *were happening* at some time in the past.

> Waldo **was trying** to walk up the down escalator.

> We **were playing** football when the rain started.

**3**

## Main Verbs and Helping Verbs (continued)

The helping verbs *have, has,* and *had* are used with main verbs that usually end with *ed.* This pattern is used to tell about things that have *already happened.*

> She **has looked** everywhere for her pet grasshopper.
>
> They **have worked** on this project for a week.
>
> He **had finished** feeding his giraffe before we got there.

## Linking Verbs

So far, most of the main verbs we have seen have been **action verbs**: *look, try, play, work.* These verbs told us that the subject was *doing* something. There is another kind of verb that does not express action, but it does connect the subject with more information in the predicate of the sentence. This is called a **linking verb**.

> Kim **is** a good student. She **seems** very happy today.

---

- A **linking verb** is a verb that connects the subject of the sentence to the words in the predicate. Often the predicate contains *nouns* that tell what the subject *is*. The predicate may also contain *adjectives* that describe the subject. (*Adjectives* are discussed in Chapter 4.)
- The verb *be* is often used as a linking verb.

---

## ● Linking Verbs
### (continued)

In the next sentences the predicate tells what the subject *is*, not what it does. Each predicate begins with a **linking verb** and is followed by more information about the subject.

My pet mouse **is** my best friend.

They **are** my next-door neighbors.

I **am** in the fourth grade at school.

We **are** glad that the storm didn't do much damage.

In these sentences you see that *is, are,* and *am* are the **main verbs**. (On page 53 you saw these same words used as *helping verbs* when they were followed by a *main verb.)* All these words are forms of the verb *be*. This verb is often used as a **linking verb**. It allows the predicate to give more information about the subject.

## ● Irregular Verbs

Some verbs do not follow the patterns that we saw in regular verbs. Verbs with their own special patterns are called **irregular verbs**. Most irregular verbs do not simply add *ed* in the past tense. Instead, they use completely *different spellings* in the present tense and the past tense.

# ● Irregular Verbs (continued)

## • THE VERB *BE* IN THE PRESENT TENSE

The verb *be* is one of the most irregular verbs in the language. It has its own special patterns in the present tense as well as the past tense.

**PRESENT TENSE**

|   | Singular | Plural |
|---|----------|--------|
| 1. | I am | we are |
| 2. | you are | you are |
| 3. | he is | they are |
|   | she is |  |
|   | it is |  |

Notice that the base form *be* does not appear at all in the present tense. However, the word *be* is used in other tenses, as you will see later.

When a form of this word is used as a **linking verb**, it is the main verb in the sentence.

I **am** nine years old and I **am** in the third grade.

My dad **is** a teacher and my mom **is** a florist.

We **are** on the same team.

When a form of this word is used as a **helping verb**, it is followed by the main verb which ends with *ing.*

I **am waiting** for the bus.

We **are going** to California next summer.

She **is looking** for her pet turtle.

## ● Irregular Verbs (continued)

- ### THE VERB *BE* IN THE PAST TENSE

In the **past tense**, the verb *be* is written this way.

**PAST TENSE**

| | Singular | Plural |
|---|---|---|
| 1. | I was | we were |
| 2. | you were | you were |
| 3. | he was | they were |
| | she was | |
| | it was | |

The word *was* is used after *I* and after the pronouns *he, she, it,* or a singular noun. The word *were* is used in all the other forms. The following examples use the past tense of the verb *be* as the main verb of each sentence:

I **was** glad when my cat had kittens.

We **were** members of the same team.

You **were** the first one to finish the test.

My friend Fred **was** frozen with fright.

- ### THE VERB *BE* IN THE FUTURE TENSE

Here the verb *be* follows the same pattern seen in regular verbs. The base form *be* is combined with the helping verb *will*, just as in other verbs in the future tense.

**FUTURE TENSE**

| | Present | Past |
|---|---|---|
| 1. | I will be | we will be |
| 2. | you will be | you will be |
| 3. | he will be | they will be |
| | she will be | |
| | it will be | |

# Irregular Verbs (continued)

## • THE VERB *HAVE* IN THE PRESENT TENSE

*Have* is another irregular verb that we use very often. This is the way *have* is written in the present tense:

**PRESENT TENSE**

| | Singular | Plural |
|---|---|---|
| 1. | I have | we have |
| 2. | you have | you have |
| 3. | he has | they have |
| | she has | |
| | it has | |

Here the word *has* is the form that is different from the others. *Has* is used only after the pronouns *he, she, it,* or a singular noun. The base form *have* is used everywhere else.

Earlier we saw that *have* and *has* could be used as helping verbs. Now we are looking at *have* as the main verb in the sentence. When it is used this way, it often means that someone *owns* something *(My cousin has red hair)*. It can also be used to mean to *contain* or *consist* of something *(An hour has sixty minutes)*.

The following sentences were written by students your age. They show how the words *have* and *has* are used in the present tense.

My family **has** three dogs and two cats.

I **have** a new bike and it's really great.

We **have** a gerbil at our school.

I **have** five people in my family.

My sister **has** brown hair, brown eyes, and freckles.

In school we **have** a class library.

## ● Irregular Verbs (continued)

- • THE VERB *HAVE* IN THE PAST TENSE

The verb *have* changes to *had* in the past tense. This spelling is used with all subjects, singular or plural.

**PAST TENSE**

|     | Singular | Plural   |
|-----|----------|----------|
| 1.  | I had    | we had   |
| 2.  | you had  | you had  |
| 3.  | he had   | they had |
|     | she had  |          |
|     | it had   |          |

The following sentences use this verb in the past tense:

My friend **had** a bad cold.

We **had** a lot of fun when we went to Ohio.

My grandfather **had** two horses and a cow.

I **had** an accident, and my mom **had** a fit.

- • THE VERB *HAVE* IN THE FUTURE TENSE

In the future tense, this verb follows the regular pattern. The base form *have* is combined with the helping verb *will*.

**FUTURE TENSE**

|     | Singular     | Plural        |
|-----|--------------|---------------|
| 1.  | I will have  | we will have  |
| 2.  | you will have| you will have |
| 3.  | he will have | they will have|
|     | she will have|               |
|     | it will have |               |

**3**

## ● Irregular Verbs (continued)

### • SOME OTHER IMPORTANT IRREGULAR VERBS

The following list shows some irregular verbs that are often used. Each verb is written in the **present tense** in the first column. In the second column the verb is written in the **past tense**. Notice that not one of these irregular verbs adds *ed* to form the past tense. The third column gives the form of the verb that is used after the helping verbs *have, has,* or *had*. Often this spelling is different from the other two.

| PRESENT | PAST | PAST with *have, has,* or *had* |
| --- | --- | --- |
| do, does | did | done |
| go, goes | went | gone |
| make, makes | made | made |
| come, comes | came | come |
| see, sees | saw | seen |
| run, runs | ran | run |
| sell, sells | sold | sold |
| fly, flies | flew | flown |
| sing, sings | sang | sung |
| swim, swims | swam | swum |
| begin, begins | began | begun |
| grow, grows | grew | grown |
| throw, throws | threw | thrown |
| buy, buys | bought | bought |
| bring, brings | brought | brought |
| take, takes | took | taken |
| give, gives | gave | given |
| eat, eats | ate | eaten |
| hide, hides | hid | hidden |
| write, writes | wrote | written |
| take, takes | took | taken |
| ride, rides | rode | ridden |

# ● Irregular Verbs (continued)

## • USING IRREGULAR VERBS

The following sentences show how to use the irregular verbs *come, see, run, sing, swim, begin, buy,* and *bring*. These sentences show which spelling to use in the *past tense* and which to use with the helping verbs *have, has,* or *had:*

> Yesterday the repairman **came** to fix the furnace. He **has come** three times this winter.
> I **saw** a lot of snakes and lizards at the zoo. I **had seen** some of them on earlier visits.
> My brother **ran** in a race last Saturday. He **has run** in several races this past year.
> The soloist **sang** very well. She **has sung** with our choir before.
> Yesterday the ducks **swam** in the pond in the park. They **have swum** all the way across many times.
> The meeting **began** on time yesterday. Most of the meetings **have begun** on time since I've been going to them.
> Scott **bought** another skateboard yesterday. He **has bought** three of them this year, and he has broken all of them.
> My grandparents **brought** a lot of stuff on their last visit. They **have brought** gifts on their last three visits.

## • DOUBLING CONSONANTS

Look back at the last seven verbs on page 60. Each of these verbs adds the ending *en* when it is used after the helping verbs *have, has,* or *had*. Also notice that the final consonant is doubled in *hidden, written,* and *ridden*.

> We **hid** behind the old barn. We **have hidden** there many times before, and we've never been found.
> My friend **wrote** a letter to me last week. He **has written** several times since he moved away.
> I **rode** a pony the last time I went to the fair. I **have ridden** ponies before.

**3**

# ✓ CHECK YOUR UNDERSTANDING
### ANSWERS BEGIN ON PAGE 231.

## Recognizing Verbs

*You may want to write the answers on a separate sheet of paper.*

**1.** Underline the **verb** in each sentence.

1. The wind scattered the leaves all over the yard.

2. She celebrates her birthday today.

3. The house shakes in bad storms.

4. My teeth chatter in cold weather.

5. Can you pronounce these words?

**2.** Look at the list of verbs given here:

perform    describe    prepare    complain    spend

Use one of these verbs in each blank space in the following sentences.

1. Does he always ___ when he falls in the mud?

2. Try not to ___ all the money in one place.

3. Can you ___ the way he looked?

4. I must ___ for the test tomorrow.

5. We will ___ in the school play next week.

➡ *If you have trouble with any of these, talk to your parent or teacher.*

# CHECK YOUR UNDERSTANDING

## Verbs in the Present Tense

*You may want to write the answers on a separate sheet of paper.*

**1.** Add the correct form of the verb in the blank space. Here is an example:

> I watch. He ____. (He **watches**.)

> 1. You wish. She ____.

> 2. They catch. He ____.

> 3. I cough. He ____.

> 4. We buy. They ____.

> 5. She arrives. You _____.

**2.** Choose the correct form of the verbs given in parentheses.

> 1. My pet monster (call, calls) me all sorts of names.

> 2. You (run, runs) faster than Tom's turtle does.

> 3. Ann (push, pushes) her little sister in the swing.

> 4. Felix (watch, watches) baseball games on TV.

> 5. Ellen (understand, understands) this better than I do.

**3.** Choose the verb that makes the most sense in each sentence. Be sure to add *s* or *es* to the verb if it is needed.

> 1. He (hurry, crawl) across the busy street.

> 2. She (jump, know) the answers to most of these questions.

> 3. Joan (visit, borrow) her grandparents every summer.

> 4. I often (munch, swim) in the pool near my house.

> 5. Her father (lift, fly) a jet airplane.

➡ *If you have trouble with any of these, talk to your parent or teacher.*

**3**

## ☑ CHECK YOUR UNDERSTANDING

### Verbs in the Past Tense

*You may want to write the answers on a separate sheet of paper.*

1. Tell what change you must make to write each of these verbs in the **past tense**. Then write the verb in the past tense. Here is an example:

   carry - change **y** to **i** and add **ed: carried**.

   1. smile          4. bury
   2. marry          5. plan
   3. discover       6. rescue

2. In each sentence, underline the verbs in the **past tense**.

   1. We wondered when the storm would stop.
   2. They continued their work after the game was over.
   3. He worried all day about the test.
   4. Debbie and I waited for Andy to call.
   5. She believed that she would find her lost poodle.

3. Notice that each verb in parentheses is given in its base form. Change the verb so that it will be in the **past tense**.

   1. We (hurry) home from school yesterday.
   2. They (stop) the game because of the weather.
   3. The hamster (race) around in his cage last night.
   4. We (carry) as many books as we could.
   5. Erica (describe) what happened yesterday.

➥ *If you have trouble with any of these, talk to your parent or teacher.*

# CHECK YOUR UNDERSTANDING ✓

## The Irregular Verbs *be* and *have*

*You may want to write the answers on a separate sheet of paper.*

**1.** Use the correct form of the verb *be* in each blank space. Notice that some sentences require the *present tense* and some require the **past tense.**

    1. Yesterday I ___ outside playing in the leaves.

    2. Today she ___ one of my best friends.

    3. Earlier, my friends ___ in the next room.

    4. Now he ___ upstairs looking for his frog.

**2.** Use the correct form of the verb *have* in each blank space. Use the **present tense** or the **past tense** as indicated by the wording of the sentence.

    1. Today I ___ a lot of homework to do.

    2. Yesterday they ___ a good time at the zoo.

    3. Last week you ___ good luck when you found your money.

    4. Now Sue ___ the bike she always wanted.

**3.** Correct the mistakes in the use of the verbs *be* and *have.*

    1. I **has** more work than I can finish.

    2. She **are** not as good at math as I am.

    3. You **was** the first one to see them.

    4. John **have** many different kinds of notebooks.

    5. They **was** upstairs playing with the dragon.

➥ *If you have trouble with any of these, talk to your parent or teacher.*

**3**

# ☑ CHECK YOUR UNDERSTANDING

## Irregular Verbs in the Past Tense
*You may want to write the answers on a separate sheet of paper.*

1. Each of these sentences contains a verb in its base form. Use this verb in the **past tense** in each sentence. Here is an example:

    I **see** the snow fall.  I **saw** the snow fall.

    1. John **do** his homework before dinner last night.

    2. Tina's pet rock **run** away from home again.

    3. She **give** a party for her scout troop last Saturday.

    4. We **buy** new shoes for my brother and his pet camel.

    5. You **go** to the park last Saturday, didn't you?

2. Here is a list of verbs in their base forms:

    say   come   take   go   see

    Use one of these verbs in the **past tense** to fill in the blank in each sentence.

    1. We ____ the wind blow the old tree down last night.

    2. My friends _____ to visit me last week.

    3. They ____ the package would arrive yesterday.

    4. Tom and Ann ____ their little brother to the mall yesterday.

    5. We _____ to California on vacation last summer.

3. Correct the errors in these sentences. Each verb should be in the **past tense**.

    1. Who **bring** these cookies?

    2. I know we **buy** more potato chips than this.

    3. She **say** we could play with the gopher.

    4. We **sell** lots of lemonade last week when it was hot.

➥ *If you have trouble with any of these, talk to your parent or teacher.*

# CHECK YOUR UNDERSTANDING

## Verbs in the Future Tense

*You may want to write the answers on a separate sheet of paper.*

1. Each verb is written in the present tense. Write the same verb in the **past tense** and the **future tense**.

| PRESENT | PAST | FUTURE |
|---|---|---|
| 1. We see. | We ___. | We ___ ___. |
| 2. They run. | They ___. | They ___ ___. |
| 3. I do. | I ___. | I ___ ___. |
| 4. You buy. | You ___. | You ____ ____. |
| 5. She is. | She ____. | She ____ ____. |

2. Look at this list of verbs:   tell   give   run   stop
   Choose a verb from the list and write the verb in the **future tense** in each of these sentences.

   1. I ___ ___ you some of my cake at lunchtime.

   2. They ____ ___ in the race tomorrow.

   3. The bus ___ ___ at the next corner.

   4. John ___ ___ us the story he just heard.

3. Each of these sentences is written in the past tense. Change the verb to the **future tense**. Here is an example:

   We dropped all the mirrors. We **will drop** all the mirrors.

   1. We saw a movie about teenage mutant ninja turkeys.

   2. He went to the mall with his friends.

   3. They shopped for a new doghouse.

   4. My cat watched for the postman.

   5. She fell seven times on the ice.

➥ *If you have trouble with any of these, talk to your parent or teacher.*

**3**

# ✓ CHECK YOUR UNDERSTANDING

## Helping Verbs

*You may want to write the answers on a separate sheet of paper.*

**1.** Choose the correct **helping verb** from those shown in parentheses.

1. I (has, have) eaten twelve bananas.

2. I (has, have) called three times already.

3. She (has, have) looked everywhere for her scarf.

4. We (has, have) written three letters to them.

5. It (have, has) rained every day this week.

**2.** Add the correct helping verb *have* or *has* in each blank space.

1. He _____ played ball with them all summer.

2. I _____ walked up and down the street for an hour.

3. John and Mark _____ been friends all week.

4. Maria _____ painted a beautiful picture.

5. We _____ written letters to our friends.

➡ *If you have trouble with any of these, talk to your parent or teacher.*

68

# Adjectives and Adverbs
## Words That Describe Other Words

Look at these two sentences. What happens when the words in boldface are added?

The elephant climbed up the hill.

The **old** elephant **slowly** climbed up the **steep** hill.

The first sentence says what the elephant did, but the second sentence gives much more information. Two of the words in boldface described *nouns* (the ***old*** elephant, the ***steep*** hill), and the other word in boldface described the *verb* (***slowly*** climbed).

The words in boldface are called **modifiers**. The word *modify* means "to change." In language, *modifiers* change other words by making the meaning of those words more definite. The boldface words changed the nouns and the verb of the sentence by telling the reader *more* about these words.

In this chapter we will look at two important kinds of modifiers: **adjectives** and **adverbs**.

## ADJECTIVES

- An **adjective** is a word that describes a *noun* or a *pronoun*.

Adjectives are often placed just before the nouns they modify. Many adjectives tell *what kind* of thing we are describing. Other adjectives tell *how many* or *how much* we are talking about.

##  Adjectives That Tell *What Kind*

Adjectives can describe the *size* or *shape* of things. All the names of *colors* can be used as adjectives. Other adjectives describe the way things *feel* or *sound*. The adjectives in the following sentences tell *what kind* of thing we are talking about:

A **gray** squirrel was chasing a **white** poodle.

The house had **round** windows and a **square** door.

I saw the skeleton of a **gigantic** dinosaur in the museum.

The hummingbird is an extremely **small** bird.

The **soft** blanket felt very good.

A **warm** breeze blew in from the ocean.

I scraped my arm on the **rough** bark of that tree.

The old table still has a **smooth** surface.

The **loud** noise scared me.

I liked that **soft** music very much.

The siren made a **shrill** sound.

I wish someone would fix that **squeaky** door.

Can you find the adjectives in these sentences?

We have a big kitchen and a little dining room.

Turk is a brown dog with a white spot on his chest.

My favorite sports are football and baseball.

When I woke up I heard a strange sound.

Did you pick out *big* and *little* in the first sentence and *brown* and *white* in the second sentence? Did you find *favorite* in the third sentence and *strange* in the last sentence? These were the adjectives in these four sentences. Each adjective was followed by the noun it modified.

## ● Adjectives That Tell *How Many* or *How Much*

When we tell how many things we are talking about, we often use the words that name *numbers*. We can use those words that tell *exactly* how many things there are *(one, two, three)*. We can also use the numbers that indicate the *order* in which things occur *(first, second, third)*. When these words are used as adjectives, they are often placed just before nouns they modify.

**One** giraffe and **three** monkeys escaped from the zoo.

There are **two** things I don't like about living on a farm.

Maria is always the **first** student to finish the test.

There are **nine** players on a baseball team.

Some other adjectives give a general idea of how many things we are talking about. These are less specific than the number words, as you see in the following examples.

We found **many** leaves in the park.

He looked at a **few** gorillas in the pet store.

Susan brought **several** things to show us.

**4**

The following adjectives also give an idea of *how much*. These adjectives describe general categories.

The storm did **much** damage to the older trees.

I still have **many** friends in my old neighborhood.

That car was involved in a **serious** accident.

There is an **enormous** chipmunk in my yard.

## The Adjectives *a, an,* and *the*

These three adjectives are so important that they have a special name of their own.

- The adjectives *a, an,* and *the* are called **articles**.

The words *a* and *an* refer to *any* person or thing.

### Use *a* before singular nouns that begin with a consonant.

I have **a** cold. She wants **a** pet raccoon.

### Use *an* before singular nouns that begin with a vowel.

She lost **an** umbrella. He found **an** elephant.

The word *the* indicates the *particular* thing or things you are talking about. **Use *the* with singular or plural nouns.**

In the following sentences, *a* and *an* indicate *any* thing. The word *the* tells exactly which thing we are talking about.

Here is **a** book. That is exactly **the** book I wanted.

She wanted **a** dog. This is **the** dog she chose.

Mom lost **an** umbrella. We found **the** umbrella she lost.

The articles can also be used with other adjectives to tell more about nouns. Here are some examples:

I have **a** bike. It is **a new red** bike.

They took **a** test. It was **an easy** test.

He ate **an** apple. It was **a big green apple**.

## Using Adjectives in the Predicate of the Sentence

So far you have seen adjectives that were placed directly before the nouns they described.

I have a **beautiful** dog.

Adjectives may also be used *after* the nouns they describe.

My dog is **beautiful**.

> • Adjectives can be used in the predicate near the end of the sentence. When adjectives are used this way, they are placed after **linking verbs**. The linking verb separates the adjective from the noun it describes.

Here are a few more sentences that contain adjectives in the predicate of the sentence following a linking verb:

The blanket is **soft** and **fuzzy**.

John and Tom are very **lucky**.

This lemon is extremely **delicious**.

The game last Saturday was not very **exciting**.

When adjectives are used to describe **pronouns**, then the adjectives are placed in the predicate of the sentence following a linking verb.

He was very **happy** after he won the race.

They were **tired** after their long trip.

You can see how these adjectives tell what the subject pronoun *is*. It would be very odd to place these adjectives before the pronoun; you would not expect to read about a *happy he* or *tired they*.

## ● Using Adjectives to Compare Things

Adjectives can describe individual people or places or things. They can also be used to *compare* two or more people or places or things. Here are the endings that are added to most adjectives when they are used to make comparisons:

- When you compare two things, add *er* to the base form of most adjectives.

  Bill is **taller** than John.

  Texas is **bigger** than Maine.

- When you compare more than two things, add *est* to the base form of most adjectives.

  She is the **youngest** student in the class.

  Alaska is the **biggest** state in the country.

Did you notice that the adjectives in these sentences came *after* the linking verbs *is* ? This will often happen when you use these adjectives to make comparisons.

# Using Adjectives to Compare Things
## (continued)

- ## SPELLING ADJECTIVES THAT END WITH *ER* AND *EST*

Many adjectives can add *er* or *est* without any other change in spelling. This is especially true with adjectives that end with *two consonants*.

| | |
|---|---|
| dark, darker, darkest | light, lighter, lightest |
| long, longer, longest | short, shorter, shortest |
| fast, faster, fastest | high, higher, highest |
| warm, warmer, warmest | tall, taller, tallest |
| cold, colder, coldest | small, smaller, smallest |

- ## ADJECTIVES THAT DOUBLE THE FINAL CONSONANT WITH *ER* AND *EST*

Most adjectives add *er* and *est* to make comparisons. If adjectives end with a *single vowel* and a *single consonant,* then you must double the final consonant before you add *er* and *est.* Here are some adjectives that double the final consonant in the base word when they are used to make comparisons:

| | |
|---|---|
| bi**g**, bi**gg**er, bi**gg**est | hot, hotter, hottest |
| wet, wetter, wettest | flat, flatter, flattest |
| sad, sadder, saddest | thin, thinner, thinnest |

# Using Adjectives to Compare Things
## (continued)

- ADDING *ER* AND *EST* TO ADJECTIVES THAT END WITH *E*

Some adjectives end with the letter **e.** We have already seen that this final **e** is dropped before we add any ending that begins with a vowel. Here are some examples of adjectives that drop the final **e** before adding **er** and **est:**

| | |
|---|---|
| nice, nic**er**, nic**est** | wide, wider, widest |
| ripe, riper, ripest | brave, braver, bravest |
| pale, paler, palest | tame, tamer, tamest |
| fine, finer, finest | large, larger, largest |

- ADDING *ER* AND *EST* TO ADJECTIVES THAT END WITH *Y*

When adjectives end with a consonant and **y**, this final **y** must be changed to **i** before we add **er** and **est.**

| | |
|---|---|
| eas**y**, eas**ier**, eas**iest** | busy, busier, busiest |
| lazy, lazier, laziest | heavy, heavier, heaviest |
| funny, funnier, funniest | happy, happier, happiest |
| lucky, luckier, luckiest | steady, steadier, steadiest |
| fancy, fancier, fanciest | sleepy, sleepier, sleepiest |

# Using Adjectives to Compare Things
## (continued)

- MAKING COMPARISONS WITH *MORE* AND *MOST*

Not all adjectives can simply add the **er** and **est** endings when they are used to make comparisons. Many adjectives with *more than one syllable* must be handled differently.

With these words, comparisons are made by adding *more* or *most* before the adjective to show an *increase* in quantity.

---

- *More* **is used before the adjective when you compare only two things**.

    This test is **more difficult** than the last one.

    This book is **more interesting** than that one.

---

- *Most* **is used before the adjective when you compare more than two things**.

    This is the **most difficult** test I ever took.

    This is the **most interesting** book I ever read.

---

The adjectives *difficult* and *interesting* are two of the words that use *more* and *most* to make comparisons. The next sentences show some other adjectives that must be combined with *more* and *most* to make comparisons.

These flowers are **more beautiful** than those.

Mike's mouse is **more musical** than Mindy's moose.

This chair is **more comfortable** than that one.

My frog is the **most intelligent** animal on my block.

This is the **most exciting** movie I've ever seen.

That was the **most expensive** coat in the store.

# Using Adjectives to Compare Things
### (continued)

• MAKING COMPARISONS WITH *LESS* AND *LEAST*

On the preceding page you saw adjectives that used the words *more* and *most* to make comparisons. These same adjectives use the words *less* and *least* to show a *decrease* in quantity.

---

• *Less* **is used before the adjective when you compare only two things.**

> This trip was **less tiring** than the one last summer.

> Your dog is **less frightened** than mine is.

---

• *Least* **is used before the adjective when you compare more than two things.**

> That is the **least interesting** show on TV.

> This is the **least difficult** test we've had so far.

---

On the bottom of page 77 you saw some sentences using *more* and *most*. If we change to the words *less* and *least,* those same sentences have the opposite meaning.

> These flowers are **less beautiful** than those.

> Mike's mouse is **less musical** than Mindy's moose.

> This chair is **less comfortable** than that one.

> My frog is the **least intelligent** animal on my block.

> This is the **least exciting** movie I've ever seen.

> That was the **least expensive** coat in the store.

# Using Adjectives to Compare Things
## (continued)

- MAKING COMPARISONS WITH *GOOD* AND *BAD*

The adjectives *good* and *bad* have their own special pattern when they are used to make comparisons.

---

- **The words *good, better,* and *best* are the forms of the adjective *good*.**

  Use **good** to describe one thing.
  I think this is a **good** pizza.

  Use **better** to compare two things.
  John believes that he has a **better** pizza.

  Use **best** to compare more than two things.
  Mary says that she has the **best** pizza of all.

---

- **The words *bad, worse,* and *worst* are the forms of the adjective *bad*.**

  Use **bad** to describe one thing.
  We had a **bad** storm last night.

  Use **worse** to compare two things.
  That storm was **worse** than the one last week.

  Use **worst** to compare more than two things.
  The storm in April was the **worst** one we've had all year.

---

## Proper Adjectives

The following sentences use **proper nouns** to name specific countries or cities. Proper nouns are always capitalized.

> Many people came from **England** to **America**.
>
> **Boston** is a large city in the northeast.

Now look at these sentences:

> **English** sheep dogs are large and hairy.
>
> An **American** flag waved over the building.
>
> The **Boston** terrier is not a very big dog.

These sentences used the names of countries and cities as **proper adjectives**.

> • A **proper adjective** is made from a proper noun. Proper adjectives are always capitalized.

Sometimes a proper noun can be used as a proper adjective without any change in spelling. For example, we can talk about a *Boston terrier* or a *California condor*. However, it is usually necessary to change the ending of the proper noun when we use it as a proper adjective.

The endings *-an, -ian, -ish,* and *-ese* are often used to change proper nouns to proper adjectives. On the next page you will see some proper nouns that become proper adjectives when these endings are used.

| NOUN | ADJECTIVE | NOUN | ADJECTIVE |
|------|-----------|------|-----------|
| America | American | England | English |
| Rome | Roman | Spain | Spanish |
| Alaska | Alaskan | Britain | British |
| Paris | Parisian | China | Chinese |
| Canada | Canadian | Japan | Japanese |

# Using Adjectives in Sentences

The following sentences were written by students your age. These sentences use many of the adjectives we have talked about. Some of them show how to use *more* and *most*, *less* and *least*. Others use *bad, worse,* and *worst*.

Our team scored **more** points than the other team.

Soccer is the **most exciting** sport to play.

I asked which was the **least expensive** boat.

I have a very **good** dog. She is the **best** dog in the world.

He likes to watch TV with his **best** friend.

The news said there would be a **bad** storm.

This is the **worst** day I have ever had.

Summer days are usually **nice**. Sometimes they are too **hot**.

The weather was **chilly** and **damp**.

My **best** friend is very **nice** and **helpful**.

This game was **less interesting** than the first one.

Every day the weather was **worse** than the day before.

In these sentences, many adjectives appear just before the nouns they describe. The last five sentences contain adjectives in the *predicate* after linking verbs.

# ADVERBS

We have just seen how adjectives can be used to tell more about nouns or pronouns. There is another group of words that can be used as modifiers, too. These words are called **adverbs**.

> • An **adverb** is a word that tells more about a *verb*.

Sometimes adverbs are used to modify adjectives and other adverbs. For now we will concentrate on adverbs that modify verbs. Adverbs are often used to tell *when* an action happened. They can also be used to tell *how* or *where* it happened.

## Adverbs That Tell *When*

The following sentences were written by students your age. In each sentence, the verb tells *what happened* and the adverb tells *when* it happened. The adverbs are written in boldface.

I **always** become dizzy on the roller coaster.

They are going to race **again** this year.

**Sometimes** he scores the most points.

I **always** want them to pick me for the team.

And **then** my dad came in to wake me for school.

We get to stay in at recess **sometimes**.

Here are a few more sentences showing how adverbs can tell *when* something happened. Notice that some adverbs come *before* the verb they modify and other adverbs come *after* the verb they modify.

We visit my grandparents very **often**.

We waited an hour, but they **never** arrived.

**Once** I saw the Grand Canyon from an airplane.

I **never** want to see another orange alligator in  this house.

## Adverbs That Tell *How*

In the next group of sentences you can see adverbs that tell *how* something happened:

The boat **slowly** drifted down the river.

The audience watched **quietly** because the movie was very sad.

The crowed laughed **loudly** at the clowns in the circus.

My friends arrived **safely** back home after a long trip.

We finished **easily** before the hour was up.

They picked **carefully** through the broken glass.

His pet turtle jumped **quickly** through the hoop.

## Adverbs That Tell *Where*

In these sentences, the adverbs in boldface tell *where* something happened:

I couldn't find the ball **here** by the house.

Maybe it's over **there** in your yard.

The sign says that the next town is very **near**.

The museum is not very **far** from here.

We saw the whales come **up** for air.

The truck rolled **down** to the bottom of the hill.

## Recognizing Adverbs

Adverbs can be used to answer questions about *how* or *when* or *where* something happened. This is one way you can recognize adverbs.

**How** did the squirrel run up the tree? It ran **quickly**.

**How** did they laugh at the clowns? They laughed **loudly**.

**When** did they arrive? They arrived **early**.

**When** do they go to the zoo? **Sometimes** they go to the zoo.

**Where** is my octopus? It is **here** on the sofa.

- THE WORD *VERY*

We often use *very* as an adverb, but this word does not modify a verb. Instead, *very* can be used before *adjectives* to make their meaning more intense.

> It was a **very** hot day.

> The sun was **very** warm.

*Very* can also be used to modify other adverbs.

> They left **very** early.

> We walked **very** quietly up the stairs.

- ADVERBS THAT END WITH *-LY*

Adjectives and adverbs are both modifiers, but adjectives are used *only* to describe nouns and pronouns. Adverbs are used to describe verbs and sometimes adjectives and other adverbs.

In this sentence an adjective describes a noun:

> I enjoyed the **soft** music.

Now look at the word in boldface in the next example. The word *soft* is now used to tell *how* the music was *played*.

> The music played **softly** in the background.

Many adjectives can be changed to adverbs by adding *-ly*. This happened with the adjective *soft*, which became the adverb *softly* when *-ly* was added. Here are a few more examples of adjectives that can be changed to adverbs.

ADJECTIVE + *ly* = ADVERB
proud ...............proudly
safe .................safely
bright ..............brightly
patient .............patiently

## Adverbs Used Very Often

Here are some adverbs we frequently use to tell *how*, *when*, and *where* things happen. When an adverb ends with *-ly*, look for the adjective that forms the base of the word.

| HOW | WHEN | WHERE |
|---|---|---|
| happily | now | up |
| slowly | then | down |
| easily | soon | here |
| quietly | always | there |
| safely | early | near |
| quickly | next | far |
| carefully | sometimes | outside |
| softly | today | inside |
| loudly | yesterday | ahead |
| angrily | already | behind |

When an adjective ends with *y*, change this *y* to *i* before adding *-ly* (*happy, happily*).

- USING *GOOD* AND *WELL*

These two words must be used carefully. *Good* is an adjective and should always describe a noun or pronoun.

We had a **good** time. He is a **good** pitcher.

*Well* can be an adverb when it is used after an *action verb* that describes how something is *done*.

The team played very **well** today.

*Well* can be an adjective when it is used after a *linking verb* to tell how someone *feels* or how something *is*.

I feel very **well** today. (OR: I am very **well** today.)

# Using Adverbs to Make Comparisons

- ADVERBS THAT ADD *ER* AND *EST*

Adverbs can be used to compare two actions or more than two actions. Some short adverbs can add *er* and *est*, just as adjectives did.

> My dog runs **fast**, but Susan's dog runs **faster**. Bill's dog runs the **fastest** of all.

Here are some more adverbs that add *er* and *est* when they are used to make comparisons:

> soon, sooner, soonest
> late, later, latest
> hard, harder, hardest
> high, higher, highest
> loud, louder, loudest
> deep, deeper, deepest
> long, longer, longest

Some of these words can be used as adjectives *or* adverbs. Just remember that adjectives modify nouns or pronouns; adverbs modify verbs, adjectives, or other adverbs.

> That is a very **deep** hole. (adjective)
>
> They dived very **deep** into the ocean. (adverb)
>
> That was the **loudest** noise I ever heard. (adjective)
>
> Steve cheered **loudest** of anyone at the game. (adverb)

# ⬤ Using Adverbs to Make Comparisons
## (continued)

- USING *MORE* AND *MOST*, *LESS*, AND *LEAST*

Most adverbs do not add **er** or **est** when they make comparisons. Instead, they use *more* or *most*. Longer adverbs, especially those ending with **-ly**, must use *more* and *most* to make comparisons.

> I lifted the heavy rock **easily**, but Mitchell lifted it **more easily** than I did.

> The children played **quietly** in the corner. Susan played **most quietly** of all.

These same adverbs must be used with *less* and *least* when we want to show a decrease in activity.

# ⬤ Using Adverbs in Sentences

Here are sentences that use some of the adverbs we have seen. Each adverb is written in **boldface.**

> I think I saw your gloves **outside** on the fence.

> My friends had **already** arrived before I got there.

> We could **hardly** see through the thick smoke

> They **finally** finished the job.

> The clouds **slowly** drifted away after the rain stopped.

> A crowd of a hundred people was **there**.

> We went to see them **yesterday**.

> **Suddenly** everybody looked up at the sky.

> **Then** the people left the stadium.

**4**

# CHECK YOUR UNDERSTANDING ☑

### ANSWERS BEGIN ON PAGE 238.

## Recognizing Adjectives

*You may want to write answers on a separate piece of paper.*

**1.** Underline all the adjectives you find in each sentence. Draw an arrow from each adjective to the noun it modifies.

    1. That was an easy test.

    2. He ate four bananas, two pizzas, and an apple.

    3. This little hamster is my favorite animal.

    4. The purple socks don't match your pink shoes.

    5. I like the gray cat  better than the brown dog.

**2.** Choose one of these adjectives to fit each blank space in the following sentences.

          happy   difficult   eleven   easy   foolish

    1. That was a _____ mistake to make.

    2. There are _____ players on a football team.

    3. She was _____ to see her cousin for a visit.

    4. It was not an _____ test, but I passed it.

    5. That was a very _____ problem to figure out.

**3.** Correct the mistakes in these sentences.

    1. They gave me a extra piece of candy.

    2. She had a apple and he had a egg.

    3. He drove a old rusty car.

    4. We found exactly a book we wanted.

    5. We asked a assistant to help us.

➡ *If you have trouble with any of these, talk to your parent or teacher.*

CHECK YOUR UNDERSTANDING

## Adjectives Ending with *er* and *est*

*You may want to write answers on a separate piece of paper.*

1. Write these adjectives on your paper. Also write each adjective with the *er* and *est* endings. Here is an example:

   sleepy, sleepier, sleepiest

   | | |
   |---|---|
   | 1. wide | 5. light |
   | 2. busy | 6. steady |
   | 3. rough | 7. calm |
   | 4. lazy | 8. noisy |

2. Underline the adjectives that compare two or more things.

   1. That was the luckiest catch I ever made.

   2. Erica's parakeet has brighter feathers than mine.

   3. The purple kangaroo is the strangest animal in the zoo.

   4. We caught a larger number of fish than they did.

   5. Have you ever seen a happier group of tadpoles?

3. Add *er* or *est* to the adjectives in boldface.

   1. This box is much **heavy** than that one.

   2. His cat has a **thick** coat than mine does.

   3. She jumped from the **high** diving board at the pool.

   4. My sister is **young** than I am.

   5. That is the **fancy** hat I ever saw.

➡ *If you have trouble with any of these, talk to your parent or teacher.*

# CHECK YOUR UNDERSTANDING

## More about Adjectives

*You may want to write answers on a separate piece of paper.*

1. Write each of the following adjectives on your paper and then use **more** to write the form of the adjective that compares two things. Use **most** to write the form of the adjective that compares more than two things. Here is an example:

    helpful, more helpful, most helpful

    1. interesting      4. remarkable

    2. beautiful      5. handsome

    3. definite      6. friendly

2. Underline the **proper adjective** in each sentence.

    1. The English language is spoken in many countries.

    2. Alaskan winters are long and cold.

    3. Their French poodle is still a puppy.

    4. The Canadian border separates Canada from America.

    5. She got a Siamese kitten for Christmas.

3. Use the correct form of the adjectives in boldface. See if each adjective compares *two* things or *more than two* things.

    1. That was the **bad** movie I ever saw.

    2. John was **lucky** than I was.

    3. Your hot dog tasted **good** than mine.

    4. Do you have an **easy** puzzle than this one?

    5. It was the **strange** story I ever read.

➡ *If you have trouble with any of these, talk to your parent or teacher.*

**4**

# ☑ CHECK YOUR UNDERSTANDING

## Adverbs

*You may want to write answers on a separate piece of paper.*

1. Underline the **adverb** in each sentence. Then draw an arrow from the adverb to the verb it describes. Here is an example:

    Fred's pet frog rested <u>comfortably</u> on the radiator.

    1. The boat finally stopped rocking up and down.

    2. We looked outside for the missing gloves.

    3. The audience clapped loudly after the concert.

    4. The crowd cheered wildly when he hit a home run.

    5. Their pet zebra slowly ate five watermelons.

2. Look at this list of adverbs.

    yesterday   carefully   quickly   usually   already

    Choose the adverb that fits the blank space.

    1. We walked ____ to get out of the rain and wind.

    2. They are _____ home from school before three o'clock.

    3. My friends left ____ for their trip back home.

    4. They had ____ finished before we got there.

    5. Pam _____ picked up the broken glass.

➡ *If you have trouble with any of these, talk to your parent or teacher.*

# Word Study

*In this chapter you will learn how to use various kinds of words to make your sentences clear and correct.*

## ● Homophones

Look at the words written in boldface in these sentences:

Do you **know** the answer? **No**, I don't.

**Their** dog is over **there** in the next yard.

Please **write** your name on the **right** side of the page.

In each sentence the words in boldface *sound* the same, but they are different in other ways. These words are **homophones**.

---

- **Homophones** are words that have the *same sound* but have *different* spellings and meanings.

---

The word *homophone* comes from the Greek language. In that language, *phone* means *sound*. Today we have other words such as *telephone* and *phonograph* that involve *sound*.

We have to be careful with homophones when we are writing. You can see that the next sentences would be confusing if the words in boldface were not spelled correctly.

John carried **two** boxes. I tried **to** carry four boxes. I had **too** many boxes. **Two** of my boxes fell down. I won't try **to** do that again. It's **too** much trouble **to** pick them up.

Now let's see how to tell these words apart.

- ## THE HOMOPHONES *TO*, *TWO*, AND *TOO*

---

## TO

**The word *to* is used in several ways.**

- *To* is followed by a **verb** when you want to tell what someone wants to do or likes to do.

    I like **to swim**.

    He wants **to see** his cousin.

- *To* is followed by a **noun** when we talk about *where we are going*. Sometimes you may use adjectives before the noun.

    Mary walked **to school**.

    Mom went **to the grocery store**.

- *To* can be followed by a noun or by an object pronoun when we talk about *giving something **to** someone*.

    I gave the books **to Jamie**.

    My parents gave a new bike **to me**.

---

## TWO

**The word *two* stands for the numeral 2, meaning *one more than one*.** Whenever you spell the word that stands for the numeral **2**, write it as *two*. This is the only way that *two* is ever used.

    I ate **two** bananas and seven cookies.

    There are **two** chairs here and three chairs over there.

    **Two** plus **two** equals four.

---

## • THE HOMOPHONES *TO*, *TWO*, AND *TOO* (CONTINUED)

---

### TOO

**The word *too* is used in only two ways.**

**1. *Too* can mean "also" or "in addition."**

I went to the store. My little brother went, **too**.

I like baseball. I like football, **too**.

She had some pizza. I had some, **too**.

**2. *Too* can mean "more than enough."**

That box is **too** heavy to carry.

It is **too** far to walk all the way home.

*Too* is often followed by *much* or *many*.

They had **too much** to eat.

We had **too many** things to do.

*Too* is also often followed by other adjectives:

| | |
|---|---|
| too heavy | too far |
| too tall | too short |
| too big | too small |
| too little | too long |

---

- ## THE HOMOPHONES *THERE* AND *THEIR*

---

- *There* means "in that place." This word is used to show that something is some distance away.

  My boots are not here. Maybe they are over **there**.

---

*There* can be contrasted with the word *here*, which shows that something is *near* or only a short distance away. *There* is usually used as an adverb.

---

- *Their* is a *possessive pronoun*. It shows that something is owned by more than one person. *Their* is used to modify a noun.

  This dog belongs to my neighbors. It is **their** dog.

---

Here are some sentences that use *there* and *their:*

My book is over **there** on that table. **Their** books are here on this desk.

**There** are the papers I have been looking for. John and Evan said that **their** papers are here on the table.

Bob and Sally and **their** parents went to New York last week. They did lots of things while they were **there**.

Do not confuse *there* and *their* with *they're,* which sounds almost the same. *They're* is a shortened form of the words *they are.*

*They're* is called a **contraction** because it *contracts* or shortens two words into one by omitting some letters. You will find out more about contractions later in this chapter.

- THE HOMOPHONES *RIGHT* AND *WRITE*

---

- ***Right*** is often used as an adjective to mean "the opposite of *left*." It shows the direction of something.

   His house is on the left side of the street and mine is on the **right** side.

- ***Right*** can also be an adjective that means "correct" or "free from mistakes." It is the opposite of *wrong*.

   Did you get the **right** answer for the third question?

   I hope I bought the **right** kind of pickles.

---

This word is spelled *right* even though the letters ***gh*** are not pronounced. Many centuries ago these letters were pronounced, and they are still used in spelling the word even though they are not spoken today. Other words have this spelling pattern: *light, night, might, sight,* and *flight.*

---

- ***Write*** is a verb which means "to mark words or symbols on paper or some other surface."

   Please **write** the answers on your paper.

   Did you **write** a letter to your grandmother?

---

When we *write* we usually use a pencil or pen and paper. We can also *write* by typing words on a typewriter or a computer and then printing them. This is the basic meaning of the word *write.*

Remember to begin this word with the letter *w.* Long ago this *w* was pronounced. Now it is silent, but we still use the spelling *write* when we talk about putting words on paper.

- ## THE HOMOPHONES *NO* AND *KNOW*

---

- *No* can mean the opposite of *yes*. It can also mean "not any."

   **No**, this is not the kind of ice cream I wanted.

   There were **no** clouds in the sky after the storm.

---

- *Know* means "to understand something" or "to be certain of your information." It can also mean "to be acquainted with someone." This is a *verb* in its base form.

   I **know** this is the right answer.

   My parents **know** some people in Chicago.

---

Long ago the *k* at the beginning of *know* was pronounced, and we still use this spelling today. Also, be careful not to confuse the words *know* and *now*. They look similar, but their pronunciations and meanings are completely different.

- ## THE HOMOPHONES *NEW* AND *KNEW*

---

- *New* is an adjective that means "not old." Something is *new* when it has existed for only a short time. It can also be *new* because we did not know about it before.

   I got some **new** gloves for Christmas.

   We found a **new** cave to explore.

---

- *Knew* is the past tense of the verb *know*.

   They **knew** we couldn't travel in such bad weather.

   I **knew** I would do well on the test.

---

- ## THE HOMOPHONES *THREW* AND *THROUGH*

---

- ### *Threw* is the past tense of the verb *throw*.

  The pitcher **threw** the ball very hard.

  I **threw** away the junk in my room.

---

- ### *Through* is used when we talk about going from the beginning to the end of something or going in one side and out the other.

  We looked **through** the whole book.

  Did he hammer the nail all the way **through** the board?

  They will travel **through** the midwest this summer.

---

In the word *through* you must remember the letters *gh* even though they are silent.

- ## SOME OTHER HOMOPHONES

  **see** - Can you **see** where they went?
  **sea** - The boat sailed across the **sea**.

  **I** - Bill and **I** are in the same class at school.
  **eye** - She looked him right in the **eye**.

  **hear** - Can you **hear** what he said?
  **here** - No one is **here** at the moment.

  **blew** - The wind **blew** some trees down.
  **blue** - The sky was very **blue** after the storm.

  **hole** - My dog dug a big **hole** in the yard.
  **whole** - My brother ate the **whole** pizza by himself.

**5**

## • SOME OTHER HOMOPHONES (CONTINUED)

**be** - Will you **be** at home this afternoon?
**bee** - The **bee** flew in the window and wouldn't leave.

**break** - Did the dishes **break** when they fell?
**brake** - The **brake** on my bike has been slipping.

**by** - Mary is standing **by** the window.
**buy** - Did you **buy** the orange shoes you saw in the store?

**wood** - This table is made of beautiful **wood**.
**would** - I **would** like to see that movie again.

**flower** - This **flower** needs some water.
**flour** - The cake used two cups of **flour**.

**nose** - My **nose** is running faster than I am.
**knows** - He **knows** where your friend is.

**week** - The weather has been nice all this **week**.
**weak** - I felt very **weak** after I had the flu.

**one** - I found only **one** of the missing pieces.
**won** - She **won** a stuffed turkey in the raffle.

**for** - This gift is **for** you.
**four** - My dog had **four** puppies and my mom had a fit.

**ate** - We **ate** dinner at our neighbor's house last night.
**eight** - I found **eight** coins in the sofa cushions.

**bear** - A large **bear** was catching fish in the stream.
**bare** - The **bare** floor is very cold in the winter.

**peace** - A period of **peace** followed the war.
**piece** - I'd like another **piece** of cake.

**steal** - The squirrels **steal** all the birdseed.
**steel** - The **steel** bridge is being painted again.

# Homographs

Look at the words in boldface in these sentences:

I **saw** a lot of birds flying south for the winter.
Is this **saw** big enough to cut these logs?

The actors took a **bow** after the performance.
I've been practicing with a **bow** and arrow.

The word *saw* has the same spelling and the same sound in each of the first two sentences. However, in the first sentence it is the past tense of the verb *see*. In the second sentence it is a noun meaning "a cutting tool with a thin blade or disc."

The word *bow* is spelled the same in each sentence of the second pair. In the first sentence it rhymes with *how* and is a noun that refers to the motion of bending at the waist as a sign of respect. In the second sentence of the pair, *bow* rhymes with *snow* and is a noun that names a weapon made from a bent strip of wood with a string attached at each end.

The words *saw* and *bow* are examples of **homographs**.

- **Homographs** are words that have the *same spelling* but have different meanings and sometimes different pronunciations.

The word *homograph* comes from the Greek language. In that language, *graph* is part of a word that means *to write*. Today we have other words such as *graphic* and *telegraph* that involve *writing* in some way.

**5**

## • USING HOMOGRAPHS

Look at these sentences using homographs. If necessary, check your dictionary to see which meaning applies in each case. Remember that some homographs will have different meanings *and* different sounds, even though they are spelled the same.

The **wind** is blowing very hard today.
Please **wind** this string into a ball.

We **wound** the garden hose into a circle.
He got a bad **wound** when he fell on the rocks.

My cat likes to **hide** under the dog.
The **hide** of the hippopotamus is very thick.

**Seal** these packages with this tape.
The **seal** was barking and clapping its flippers.

It will only take a **second** to finish the job.
This is the **second** time I've called him.

He says he **can** find what you want.
Let's open another **can** of spinach.

The sad story brought a **tear** to my eye.
Be careful not to **tear** your clothes.

The **desert** is hot and full of sand.
The mother lion won't **desert** her cubs.

The director will **lead** the next song.
This pipe is made of **lead**.

The mule can **bear** a heavy load.
I saw an enormous **bear** in the zoo.

This package has a **plain** wrapper.
The wagons traveled across the dusty **plain**.

# ⬤ Compound Words

Compare these two sentences:

Where is the **coat** that I wear in the **rain**?

Where is my **raincoat**?

It is much easier and clearer to say *raincoat* than to say "the *coat* that I wear in the *rain*." We often join two words to describe something or to give it a name that tells us what it is. The new word has a meaning of its own. When we join two shorter words to form another word, we are using **compound words**. The word *compound* means "made up of two or more parts."

> • A **compound word** is made up of two or more separate words joined together. In a compound word, each of the shorter words has its own meaning and can stand by itself.

• CLOSED COMPOUND WORDS

Many compound words are joined with no space between them. These are called **closed compound words**. You can usually tell what the compound word means if you know the meaning of the shorter words. Look for the separate words used in the following compound words. You can probably think of more compound words yourself.

| | | |
|---|---|---|
| football | railroad | notebook |
| baseball | workshop | bedroom |
| basketball | sandpaper | sunflower |
| skateboard | birthday | birdhouse |
| playground | classroom | spaceship |

## • OPEN COMPOUND WORDS

A few compound words are written as two separate words. They are still compound words because a new meaning is created when the two words are used together.

Open compound words are used in the following sentences. You can look for these compound words in your dictionary, where you will find them listed the way they are written here.

Everything is **all right**.

He says that **no one** is here.

We had a **hot dog** for lunch.

Did you have **ice cream** for dessert?

My **guinea pig** kept me awake all night.

My brother is going to **high school** next year.

## • HYPHENATED COMPOUND WORDS

Some compound words are joined by a short line called a **hyphen** (-). This short line shows that the two words are connected. Here are some hyphenated compound words that were used in compositions written by students your age:

We will leave as soon as the **baby-sitter** arrives.

I like to ride in a **go-cart**.

The **grown-ups** were talking in the next room.

Sometimes we play **hide-and-seek**.

They rode the **merry-go-round** at the fair.

When you write out the numbers from **twenty-one** through **ninety-nine**, use hyphenated compound words.

There are **twenty-seven** students in my class.

It is **forty-eight** miles to the next town.

The temperature was **eighty-four** degrees yesterday.

# Prefixes: *un-*, *dis-*, and *re-*

It is easy to understand what these sentences mean:

Will you **fold** these towels for me?

They **like** strawberry ice cream.

I must **read** that book tomorrow.

Each of the words in boldface is a base word with a definite meaning of its own. What happens to these base words when we make one small change in each of them?

Please **unfold** one of these towels.

They **dislike** vanilla ice cream.

I must **reread** this book carefully.

Now the meaning of each word in boldface has been changed because we added the letters *un-*, *dis-*, and *re-*. These letters are **prefixes**.

> - A **prefix** is a word part that is added to the *beginning* of a base word. A prefix is not a word by itself, but it changes the meaning of the base word. Prefixes do not affect the spelling of the base word.

The prefix *un-* means "not" or "the opposite of" something.

Will this key **unlock** that door?

The prefix *dis-* also means "not" or "opposite."

They always **disagree** about something.

The prefix *re-* means "again" or "back."

I want to **renew** this library book.

## Suffixes

Word parts can be added at the end of base words as well as at the beginning. Notice what happens to the words written in boldface in these sentences.

> They played **soft** music. The music played **softly**.
>
> He was willing to **help** us. He was very **helpful**.
>
> This grass has no **color**. This dead grass is **colorless**.
>
> Does she **sing** very well? Is she a good **singer**?

A base word is printed in boldface in the first sentence in each pair. Then the second sentence adds a word part at the end of each base word. We added *-ly* to the base word *soft*, *-ful* to *help*, *-less* to *color*, and *-er* to *sing*. These word parts are called **suffixes**.

> - A **suffix** is a word part added at the *end* of a base word. A suffix is not a word by itself, but it can change the way the base word is used in the sentence.

The suffix *-ly* means "in a certain way" or "to a certain extent."

The suffix *-ful* means "having the qualities of something" or "full of something" or "able to do something."

The suffix *-less* means "without" or "not having any." It is the opposite of the suffix *-ful*.

The suffix *-er* can be used to indicate the person or thing that *does* something.

- ## THE SUFFIX -*LY*

The suffix -*ly* is one that we use very often. You just saw this suffix in the word *softly*. As we pointed out in Chapter 4, the suffix -*ly* is often used to change an **adjective** to an **adverb**. Here is a list of pairs of adjectives and adverbs to remind you of this use of the suffix -*ly.*

| ADJECTIVE | ADVERB |
|---|---|
| bad | badly |
| exact | exactly |
| final | finally |
| happy | happily |
| lucky | luckily |
| easy | easily |
| perfect | perfectly |
| quick | quickly |
| slow | slowly |
| sudden | suddenly |
| usual | usually |

When the adjective ends with **y**, remember to change this **y** to **i** before you add -*ly* (*easy - easily*).

Look at the following pairs of sentences. They show words used as **adjectives** in the first sentence in each pair. Then the same word is changed to an **adverb** by adding -*ly* in the second sentence in each pair. The adjectives describe nouns, and the adverbs describe verbs.

There was a **sudden** storm. The storm blew up **suddenly**.

They were **brave** people. Those people behaved **bravely**.

This is a **slow** train. This train moves **slowly**.

He made a **perfect** catch. He caught the ball **perfectly**.

That was an **easy** job. We finished that job **easily**.

**5**

- ## THE SUFFIXES -*FUL* AND -*LESS*

Here are some pairs of sentences that use words ending with the suffixes -**ful** and -**less**. You can easily see how these suffixes affect the meaning of each base word.

> This is a very **useful** tool.
> That tool was **useless**.
>
> He was **careful** when he picked up the glasses.
> They were **careless** and dropped the dishes.
>
> These fall leaves are very **colorful**.
> The dead flowers are almost **colorless**.

These two suffixes are used to create *adjectives*. Notice that the suffix -**ful** is spelled with only one *l*. It is not the same as the separate word *full*, which ends with two *l*'s.

There are several other important words that end with -**ful**. Here are some of them.

| | |
|---|---|
| beautiful | painful |
| cheerful | wasteful |
| helpful | successful |
| playful | wonderful |

When the original word ends with a consonant followed by *y*, then this *y* must change to *i* before we add -**ful** (*beauty, beautiful*).

Sometimes we can add either -**ful** or -**less** to the same base word. This creates pairs of words with opposite meanings. You saw some of these in the sentences at the top of this page (*useful* and *useless*, for example). We can also have the words *cheerful* and *cheerless*, *helpful* and *helpless*, and *painful* and *painless*.

- THE SUFFIX -*ER*

Look at these pairs of sentences:

My dog **runs** very fast. He is a good **runner**.

They **read** many books. They are good **readers**.

They **swim** very well. They are good **swimmers**.

In the first sentence of each pair, the word in boldface is a **verb**. Each verb tells what the subject is doing. In the second sentence, -*er* has been added at the end of the verb. Now these words have become **nouns** that tell *who* or *what* is doing something.

Look at the words listed below. You can see that each verb becomes a noun when the suffix -*er* is added. The noun names the person or thing that is doing what the verb describes.

| VERB | NOUN | VERB | NOUN |
|------|------|------|------|
| bake | baker | race | racer |
| bat | batter | swim | swimmer |
| drive | driver | ride | rider |
| help | helper | win | winner |
| jump | jumper | teach | teacher |
| lead | leader | write | writer |

Remember these guidelines when you write words ending with the suffix -*er*:

- If the base word ends with *e*, drop the final *e* before the suffix -*er* is added (*bake, baker*).
- If the base word ends with a vowel and a consonant, double the final consonant before the suffix -*er* is added (*swim, swimmer*).

**5**

• THE SUFFIX -*OR*

There is another suffix that is used in some words to describe people or things that are *doing* something. Look at these sentences and see what this suffix is.

> He **sails** his boat every weekend. He is a good **sailor**.

> They will **visit** us next week. They are our **visitors**.

Here we have added **-or** instead of **-er** to name the person who is doing something. There are some other important words that end with **-or**. Although these words don't always add the suffix to a *verb*, they do name people or things that *do* something.

> doctor
> sailor
> actor
> visitor
> mayor
> author
> inventor
> governor
> investor
> reflector
> sculptor
> supervisor

Words that end with the suffixes **-er** and **-or** always add **s** to form the plural.

> All the **governors** are meeting this week.

> Several **doctors** consulted on the case.

> Most of the **actors** played their parts very well.

> Ten **sculptors** competed for the prize.

## ● Synonyms and Antonyms

Sometimes we find two or more words that mean almost the same thing.

We had a **big** dinner. We had a **large** dinner.

We had a **huge** dinner. We had an **enormous** dinner.

> • Words that mean almost the same thing are called **synonyms**.

Here are some other groups of synonyms:

| | | |
|---|---|---|
| tired, sleepy | little, small, tiny | end, finish |
| begin, start | glad, happy, joyful | bright, brilliant |

We also find groups of words that mean the opposite of each other.

We ran **up** the stairs. Then we ran **down** the stairs.

> • Words that have the opposite meaning are called **antonyms**.

Here are a few more antonyms that are often used:

| | | |
|---|---|---|
| big, little | open, close | fast, slow |
| soft, hard | tall, short | inside, outside |
| wet, dry | day, night | hot, cold |

You saw the suffixes *-ful* and *-less* on page 106. When you add these suffixes to the same base word, the words become *antonyms*.

| | |
|---|---|
| hopeful, hopeless | useful, useless |
| careful, careless | colorful, colorless |

# Words Often Confused

Some words look or sound *almost* the same, but they are actually very different in meaning. Look at the words printed in boldface in the following sentences. Notice the difference in their spelling and meaning, and be careful not to confuse them.

> We left **our** jackets at the playground.
> We **are** going to visit them next week.
>
> His frog is bigger **than** mine.
> First we looked in the attic, and **then** we looked in the basement.
>
> **When** will the party begin?
> I hope our team can **win** one more game this season.
>
> **Which** one of these bananas do you want?
> I dressed up as a **witch** for Halloween.
>
> **Where** are you going now?
> Will you **wear** your blue coat or your red one?
> We **were** planning to leave tomorrow.

Be especially careful with words that begin with the letters *wh*. These letters have the breathy /hw/ sound at the beginning of words such as *when*, *where*, and *which*. Notice the difference in the /w/ sound at the beginning of words such as *win*, *wear*, *witch*, and *were*. If you pronounce these words carefully, you can remember which begin with *w* and which begin with *wh*.

Some other words are spelled *almost* the same, but there are important differences in their meaning. You will see some of these words on the next page.

## • WORDS OFTEN CONFUSED (CONTINUED)

The words *who* and *how* contain the same letters, but the letters are written in different patterns. The same thing is true of *own* and *won*. These words don't sound the same. Be careful to write the word that has the meaning you want.

> **Who** was at the door?
> **How** did you do on the test?
>
> I **own** a new bicycle that my parents gave me.
> I **won** a new bicycle in a raffle.

It is also important to be careful with words that differ by only one letter. This is especially true with *of* and *off*, which are often confused. Also notice the difference between *an* and *and*. Be sure to spell the word that gives the meaning you want.

> Put this in front **of** the other books.
> Two books fell **off** the table.
>
> I wanted **an** apple and **an** orange.
> Ellen **and** Maria wanted to see their aunt **and** uncle.

Here are some more pairs of words that are very similar in spelling. Notice the difference in sound and meaning of these words.

| | | |
|---|---|---|
| now, know | though, thought | trial, trail |
| diary, dairy | accept, except | wonder, wander |

When you use the words *a lot,* be sure to write them as separate words. There is no such word as *alot.*

> We had **a lot** of fun.

## Contractions

Look at these pairs of sentences:

> I **do not** know where he is. I **don't** know where he is.
>
> I **am** sure he will arrive soon. **I'm** sure he will arrive soon.

There is nothing wrong with the first sentence in each pair, but the second sentence sounds more like everyday speech. Instead of saying *do not* and *I am*, we often say *don't* and *I'm*. These shortened forms are called **contractions**.

---

- A **contraction** is made up of two words combined into one. At least one letter in one of the words is left out. An **apostrophe** (') takes the place of the omitted letter.

---

## Contractions with a Verb and *Not*

One of the most important contractions involves the verb followed by the adverb *not*. This makes a *negative* statement. which says that something *did not* happen or *is not* going to happen.

---

When you write contractions involving the verb followed by *not*, the *o* in *not* is omitted and the apostrophe (') takes its place.

---

This contraction is often used with the verb *do*. It is also used with *will*, where it has an unusual change in spelling. It can also be used with verbs such as *can, could, would,* and *should*. You will see these contractions on the following pages. Later you will see how to write contractions with the irregular verbs *be* and *have*.

- CONTRACTIONS WITH *DO* AND *NOT*

Here are the spellings of the verb **do** when it is combined with **not** in the present tense:

## PRESENT TENSE

| Singular | Plural |
|---|---|
| I don't (I do not) | we don't (we do not) |
| you don't (you do not) | you don't (you do not) |
| he doesn't (he does not) | they don't (they do not) |
| she doesn't (she does not) | |
| it doesn't (it does not) | |

Here is how this contraction is written in the past tense:

## PAST TENSE

| Singular | Plural |
|---|---|
| I didn't (I did not) | we didn't (we did not) |
| you didn't (you did not) | you didn't (you did not) |
| he didn't (he did not) | they didn't (they did not) |
| she didn't (she did not) | |
| it didn't (it did not) | |

If you remember that the apostrophe takes the place of the letter **o** in **not**, you will avoid mistakes such as these:

I **do'nt** know. (I **don't** know.)

She **does'nt** plan to stay. (She **doesn't** plan to stay.)

He **did'nt** say anything. (He **didn't** say anything.)

- The contractions **don't** and **doesn't** are used in the present tense.
- The contraction **didn't** is used in the past tense.

- ## CONTRACTIONS WITH *WILL* AND *NOT*

The helping verb *will* can be combined with a main verb to form the future tense. By adding the word *not* after *will*, you can make a negative statement. If you want to say that something *will not* happen at some time in the future, you can combine these two words in a contraction.

> - ## The contraction of *will not* is always spelled *won't*.

We **won't leave** before noon tomorrow.
(We **will not leave** before noon tomorrow.)
They **won't know** the results until next Tuesday.
(They **will not know** the results until next Tuesday.)

In this contraction we must change the spelling of the *verb* itself.

| Singular | Plural |
|---|---|
| I won't (I will not) | we won't (we will not) |
| you won't (you will not) | you won't (you will not) |
| he won't (he will not) | they won't (they will not) |
| she won't (she will not) | |
| it won't (it will not) | |

The change in the spelling of *will* is necessary because it would be very difficult to pronounce *willn't* if we tried to use this as a contraction. Even though the verb itself is changed, the apostrophe still replaces the letter *o* in *not*. Notice that the spelling *won't* is used in the singular *and* the plural.

• CONTRACTIONS WITH OTHER VERBS AND *NOT*

We often combine the words ***can not*** (also spelled ***cannot***) into the contraction ***can't***. This spelling is used with all pronouns, singular and plural.

> Jane **can't** wait to see them.
>
> You **can't** get through that door.
>
> They **can't** believe what happened.

Notice that *two* letters are omitted in this contraction. We use only one *n* from *cannot*, and the apostrophe still takes the place of the *o* in *not*.

The next sentences use contractions involving the verbs *could*, *would*, and *should*.

> They **wouldn't** want you to be late.
>
> We **couldn't** wait to see his pet snake.
>
> Ellen **wouldn't** leave until the movie was over.
>
> It **shouldn't** take more than an hour to get there.

---

• **The contractions *can't*, *couldn't*, *wouldn't*, and *shouldn't* are used with all nouns and pronouns, singular and plural.**

---

Contractions involving a verb and the word *not* are often used to begin questions.

> **Isn't** your cousin coming to visit?
>
> **Hasn't** he gotten home from school yet?
>
> **Didn't** he leave a message?
>
> **Won't** you miss seeing them?
>
> **Shouldn't** we wait until they return?

## Contractions with Pronouns and Verbs

Many contractions shorten the verb itself. These are the contractions that join a pronoun with a verb. You will see these on the following pages.

- CONTRACTIONS WITH PRONOUNS AND THE VERB *BE*

The verb **be** has irregular spellings, as you know. Here is how this verb is combined with pronouns to form contractions in the present tense.

**PRESENT TENSE**

| Singular | Plural |
|---|---|
| I'm (I am) | we're (we are) |
| you're (you are) | you're (you are) |
| he's (he is) | they're (they are) |
| she's (she is) | |
| it's (it is) | |

The apostrophe took the place of the first letter in each spelling of the verb: *am*, *are*, and *is*. These contractions can be used **only in the present tense**.

There are no contractions that combine pronouns with the verbs *was* and *were* in the past tense. You must use the pronoun with the complete verb when you write *be* in the past tense.

- CONTRACTIONS WITH *BE* AND *NOT*

In the **present tense** there are two ways you can use contractions to make negative statements with the verb *be*.

---

- Add the word ***not*** after the contraction: *I'm not, you're not,* and so on.

  **I'm not** sure where he is.

  **You're not** going up there, are you?

---

- Combine the verb with the shortened form of *not*: *you aren't, he isn't, they aren't,* and so on.

  You **aren't** through with the sports section, are you?

  He **isn't** going to believe this.

  We **aren't** sure where he has gone.

  She **isn't** going to the movie tonight.

  They **aren't** coming back until next week.

---

In the **past tense** there are no contractions for the verb *be* that combine the pronoun with the verb. However, you can combine the verb with the shortened form of the word *not*.

**PAST TENSE**

| Singular | Plural |
|---|---|
| I wasn't (I was not) | we weren't (we were not) |
| you weren't (you were not) | you weren't (you were not) |
| he wasn't (he was not) | they weren't (they were not) |
| she wasn't (she was not) | |
| it wasn't (it was not) | |

- ## CONTRACTIONS WITH THE VERB *HAVE*

In the **present tense** you can combine the pronoun with shortened forms of the verb *have* to form these contractions.

### PRESENT TENSE

| Singular | Plural |
|---|---|
| I've (I have) | we've (we have) |
| you've (you have) | you've (you have) |
| he's (he has) | they've (they have) |
| she's (she has) | |
| it's (it has) | |

Notice that the contractions with the pronouns *he*, *she*, and *it* are the same with the verbs *has* and *is*. If the sentence is written clearly, you can usually tell which is intended.

> *He's* my best friend. (**He is** my best friend.)

> *She's* going to leave today. (**She is** going to leave today.)

> *He's* gone on vacation. (**He has** gone on vacation.)

> *It's* been raining all day. (**It has** been raining all day.)

In the **past tense** the contractions are written this way:

### PAST TENSE

| Singular | Plural |
|---|---|
| I'd (I had) | we'd (we had) |
| you'd (you had) | you'd (you had) |
| he'd (he had) | they'd (they had) |
| she'd (she had) | |
| it'd (it had) | |

Often you will use these contractions when *had* is a helping verb followed by a main verb.

> *I'd* waited an hour for him. (**I had** waited an hour for him.)

> *He'd* been to the dentist. (**He had** been to the dentist.)

- ## CONTRACTIONS WITH *HAVE* AND *NOT*

Here is the way to combine *have* and *not* into a contraction in the present tense:

### PRESENT TENSE

| Singular | Plural |
|---|---|
| I haven't (I have not) | we haven't (we have not) |
| you haven't (you have not) | you haven't (you have not) |
| he hasn't (he has not) | they haven't (they have not) |
| she hasn't (she has not) | |
| it hasn't (it has not) | |

In the past tense, the contraction is spelled *hadn't* with all nouns and pronouns, singular and plural.

### PAST TENSE

| Singular | Plural |
|---|---|
| I hadn't (I had not) | we hadn't (we had not) |
| you hadn't (you had not) | you hadn't (you had not) |
| he hadn't (he had not) | they hadn't (they had not) |
| she hadn't (she had not) | |
| it hadn't (it had not) | |

Remember that the apostrophe replaces the *o* in *not*. This will help you avoid mistakes like these:

I **have'nt** finished yet. (I ***haven't*** finished yet.)

It **has'nt** stopped raining. (It ***hasn't*** stopped raining.)

- The contractions ***haven't*** and ***hasn't*** are used in the present tense.
- The contraction ***hadn't*** is used in the past tense.

**5**

## • CONTRACTIONS WITH THE VERB *WILL*

The verb *will* can be combined with pronouns to form these contractions:

### PRESENT TENSE

| Singular | Plural |
|---|---|
| I'll (I will) | we'll (we will) |
| you'll (you will) | you'll (you will) |
| he'll (he will) | they'll (they will) |
| she'll (she will) | |
| it'll (it will) | |

Remember that *will* is often a helping verb that is joined with a main verb in the **future tense**. Contractions can be helpful when you are using the future tense.

> *I'll* finish this later. (**I will** finish this later.)

> *She'll* arrive tomorrow. (**She will** arrive tomorrow.)

> *We'll* see them next week. (**We will** see them next week.)

It is important to include the apostrophe when you write contractions. If you leave it out, you sometimes get a completely different word. For example, the contraction *she'll* becomes the noun *shell* if you omit the apostrophe. Also, *we'll* becomes the word *well* if you forget the apostrophe.

The past tense of *will* is *would*. This contraction is always written as **'d** after pronouns. The same contraction was used for the verb *had*. You can tell the difference if you look at the verbs which follow these contractions:

> *He'd* been away for a week. (**He had** been away for a week.)

> *He'd* like to meet them. (**He would** like to meet them.)

# Homophones That Involve Contractions

Earlier we pointed out that homophones are words which have the *same sound* but different spellings and meanings. We also mentioned that some homophones involve contractions that may be confused with other words. Here are the homophones to watch for:

it's - its
you're - your
they're - there, their

Always use the apostrophe when you write the contractions it's, you're, and they're. The other words *its*, *your*, *there*, and *their* are completely different and have their own meanings.

- ***Its*** is a possessive pronoun that shows *ownership*.
  The old car lost one of **its** wheels.
- ***It's*** is a contraction of ***it is***.
  **It's** supposed to rain all day.

---

- ***Your*** is a possessive pronoun that shows *ownership*.
  **Your** coat is in the closet.
- ***You're*** is a contraction of ***you are***.
  I hope **you're** going to like this.

---

- ***There*** is an adverb that shows the *location* of something.
  My notebook must be over **there**.
- ***Their*** is a possessive pronoun that shows *ownership*.
  John and Ellen left **their** books on the bus.
- ***They're*** is a contraction of ***they are***.
  **They're** going to leave tomorrow.

☑ **CHECK YOUR UNDERSTANDING**
ANSWERS BEGIN ON PAGE **242.**

## Homophones

*You may want to write answers on a separate piece of paper.*

**1.** Write the **homophone** that matches the sound of each word in this list.

1. see, ___          5. right, ___

2. break, ___        6. no, ___

3. nose, ___         7. by, ___

4. eye, ___          8. peace, ___

**2.** Choose the correct word from the homophones in parentheses.

1. There is enough space for (to, two) more people.

2. We (ate, eight) at a restaurant last night.

3. The weather report says (its, it's) going to snow tonight.

4. I couldn't (here, hear) what he said.

**3.** Each sentence contains a mistake. Write the correct form of the homophone.

1. Look threw these books for a picture of a dinosaur.

2. I wood like a few more peanuts.

3. Mike and Ann left there books on the bus.

4. I know its around here somewhere.

➡ *If you have trouble with any of these, talk to your parent or teacher.*

# CHECK YOUR UNDERSTANDING ☑

## Compound Words

*You may want to write answers on a separate piece of paper.*

**1.** Look at these words:  finger   earth   coat   shoe   news
cheer   water   day   book

Now join one of these words to each of the words in this list to form
a new **compound word**.

1. ___leader      4. ___paper      7. note___

2. ___fall        5. rain___       8. ___quake

3. birth___       6. ___print      9. snow___

**2.** These compound words are spelled *incorrectly*. Write the correct
spelling. Try to think of the spelling before you look for it in the
information on compound words.

1. guineapig      4. noone

2. icecream       5. alright

3. baby sitter    6. twenty seven

**3.** Use one of these compound words in each blank space in the
following sentences:

homework   hide-and-seek   all right   haircut

1. I hope you will feel _____ in the morning.

2. They are playing _____ in the park.

3. Why did she get such a short ____?

4. I finished my ___ before it got dark.

➥ *If you have trouble with any of these, talk to your parent or teacher.*

**5**

## ☑ CHECK YOUR UNDERSTANDING

### Prefixes and Suffixes

*You may want to write answers on a separate piece of paper.*

1. Underline each word that begins with a **prefix**.

   1. This is an unusual story.

   2. I don't know how all my socks could disappear.

   3. They will replay the last two minutes of the game.

   4. It took a long time to unload all the bricks.

2. When you find a word written in boldface, write it with the **suffix** that will make it fit the sentence. Here is an example:

   > The **win** of the race was very happy.
   > The **winner** of the race was very happy.

   1. They are both very good **swim**.

   2. Our **visit** will stay with us for two days.

   3. Our team **final** won a game.

   4. The storm blew up very **sudden**.

3. Underline each word that begins with a **prefix** or ends with a **suffix**.

   1. Some readers disagree with this writer.

   2. Fortunately they found all their money.

   3. The teachers were helpful to all of us.

   4. They rowed quickly back to shore.

➥ *If you have trouble with any of these, talk to your parent or teacher.*

# CHECK YOUR UNDERSTANDING

## Synonyms and Antonyms

*You may want to write answers on a separate piece of paper.*

**1.** Indicate which pairs of words are **synonyms** and which are **antonyms**.

1. light, heavy ____  4. tired, sleepy ____

2. shiny, bright ____  5. before, after ____

3. above, below ____  6. start, begin ____

**2.** Choose one of these words as a **synonym** to replace the word in boldface in each sentence.

  skinny chilly frightened breezy

1. It is a very **windy** day.

2. The new calf has very **thin** legs.

3. We were **afraid** when we listened to the ghost story.

4. It is very **cool** this evening.

**3.** Use one of these words as an **antonym** to replace the word in boldface in each sentence.

  awake difficult closed soggy

1. It was **easy** to find all the keys he dropped.

2. This pizza crust is very **crisp**.

3. Please keep the door **open**.

4. Is everyone **asleep**?

➥ *If you have trouble with any of these, talk to your parent or teacher.*

# ✓ CHECK YOUR UNDERSTANDING

## Words Often Confused

*You may want to write answers on a separate piece of paper.*

**1.** Choose the correct word from the pair of words in parentheses in each sentence.

　　1. This is (are, our) first trip to Chicago.

　　2. This stone is bigger (then, than) that one.

　　3. They said they had (alot, a lot) of fun at the zoo.

　　4. The books all fell (of, off) the table.

　　5. I don't know (were, where) I left my books.

**2.** Look at these pairs of words.

　　　　now, know　　an, and　　own, won　　wonder, wander

Choose the correct word to fit in the blank space when you write each of these sentences.

　　1. I like to _____ through the forest when the leaves fall.

　　2. Do you ___ how many cookies are left?

　　3. We saw the giraffe ___ the elephant at the zoo.

　　4. We ___ the game by two points.

　　5. I would like to have ___ apple and a banana.

➡ *If you have trouble with any of these, talk to your parent or teacher.*

# CHECK YOUR UNDERSTANDING

## Contractions

*You may want to write answers on a separate piece of paper.*

**1.** Use a contraction in place of the words in boldface.

1. **We are** going to Chicago on Saturday.

2. **He is** one of the best players on the team.

3. **She will** let us know when we should come.

4. **They have** gone on a trip.

**2.** Use a contraction in place of the words in boldface.

1. I **do not** know when they will arrive.

2. **Is not** this an interesting movie?

3. **Are not** you finished yet?

4. He **will not** finish the job until tomorrow.

**3.** These sentences were written by students your age. When you write them on your paper, use the correct contraction in place of the word in boldface.

1. I like kittens. **There** cute and easy to take care of.

2. Then he said, "**Thats** nice."

3. You can join even if **your** only nine.

4. **Shes** very nice and she likes to help children.

➡ *If you have trouble with any of these, talk to your parent or teacher.*

# Writing Better Sentences

*In this chapter you will learn more about writing various kinds of sentences. You will also learn how to find and correct mistakes in your sentences.*

## ● Compound Subjects

Look at these two sentences. How are they alike, and how are they different?

Mary saw a mysterious monster movie.

Marvin saw a mysterious monster movie.

Only the *subject* is different in each of these sentences. *Mary* is the simple subject of the first sentence, and *Marvin* is the simple subject of the second sentence. Both Mary and Marvin did the same thing: They both saw a movie.

There is nothing wrong with these sentences, but there is another way they could be written. You can join the two subjects with the word *and*. Then you can put them together in a single sentence that has a **compound subject**.

**Mary and Marvin** saw a mysterious monster movie.

> - A **compound subject** contains two or more simple subjects. These simple subjects are joined by a word such as *and*. A compound subject shows that two or more people are doing the same thing.

**6**

• MORE ABOUT COMPOUND SUBJECTS

In the next illustration you see how the two parts of the compound subject fit with the predicate.

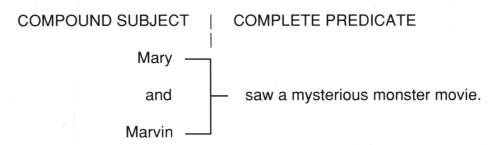

COMPOUND SUBJECT | COMPLETE PREDICATE

Mary
and      saw a mysterious monster movie.
Marvin

In the next example, the first two sentences tell about two people who did the same thing. Then the third sentence uses a compound subject to say the same thing.

**My friend** likes to play ball. I like to play ball.

**My friend and** I like to play ball.

Notice the change in the verb. In the first sentence, the singular subject *My friend* required the verb *likes*. When we use a compound subject, the verb becomes *like*.

Sometimes there are more than two parts in a **compound subject**. You can see this in the next sentences.

**Kim** wanted to leave. **Betsy** wanted to leave.
**Sue** wanted to leave.

These sentences can be combined by using a compound subject. All three names can be joined with *and*.

**Kim and Betsy and Sue** wanted to leave.

You can also use the **comma** (,) to separate the names. Then the word *and* would be used only before the last name.

**Kim, Betsy, and Sue** wanted to leave.

# ● Compound Objects

Now look at these sentences. How do they compare?

Dad played ball with Ed. Dad played ball with me.

These sentences are similar in most ways. Only one part of the predicate is different in each of them. Both sentences say that Dad played ball with someone.

The words *Ed* and *me* serve as **objects** in these sentences. They come after the verb and answer the question, "With whom was Dad playing ball?"

We can write a single sentence that joins *Ed* and *me* with the word *and*. This sentence will have a **compound object**.

Dad played ball **with Ed and me.**

> • A **compound object** contains two or more connected words. These words appear in the predicate of the sentence. They can be joined by a word such as *and*.

In the next illustration you can see how the two names at the end of the sentence form a **compound object.**

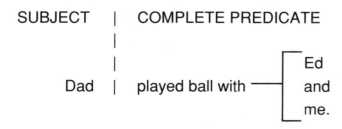

SUBJECT | COMPLETE PREDICATE

Dad | played ball with ⎡ Ed
                            and
                            ⎣ me.

**6**

• MORE ABOUT COMPOUND OBJECTS

It is also possible to join *more* than two words together in a compound object. How could you join these three sentences?

> I saw **Jane** downtown. I saw **Erica** downtown. I saw **Maria** downtown.

You can use *and* to join these names into one sentence with a **compound object**.

> I saw **Jane and Erica and Maria** downtown.

You can also use commas to separate the names. When you do this, the word *and* is used only before the last word in the compound object.

> I saw **Jane, Erica, and Maria** downtown.

# Compound Predicates

What is the same in these two sentences?

Maria found a red leaf. Maria showed it to her mother.

Here the *subject* of each sentence is the same: Maria. We can see that Maria did two things: she *found* a red leaf, and she *showed* it to her mother.

When one subject does two or more things that are related to each other, we can combine these in a sentence that has a **compound predicate**.

Maria **found a red leaf** *and* **showed it to her mother.**

> • A **compound predicate** contains two or more predicates joined by a word such as *and*. Each part of the compound predicate contains its own verb and tells that the same subject did two or more different things.

In this illustration you can see how the compound predicate is constructed.

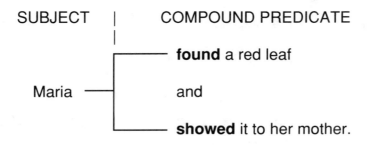

SUBJECT | COMPOUND PREDICATE

**found** a red leaf

Maria — and

**showed** it to her mother.

**6**

## • MORE ABOUT COMPOUND PREDICATES

Here is another example showing how sentences can be combined if they have the same subject:

Ellen stared at the sky. She saw a shooting star.

By using the word *and* to form a **compound predicate**, we can combine these sentences like this:

Ellen stared at the sky **and** saw a shooting star.

We don't have to repeat the subject because both parts of the predicate refer to the same person named in the subject.

Here are *three* sentences that all have the same subject:

Terry plays ball. He flies kites. He rides his bike.

A compound predicate can join all these things into one sentence. We can use *and* to connect the parts of the compound predicate, but usually it is better to use commas (,) when you write a compound predicate that contains more than two parts. Then you use *and* only before the last part of the predicate.

Terry plays ball, flies kites, and rides his bike.

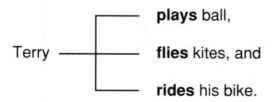

You must always be sure that the parts of the sentence belong together before you write a **compound predicate**. All parts of the predicate must have the same **subject**.

# Compound Subjects and Compound Predicates

How are these sentences alike?

Ed and I went to the store. We bought some spinach soup.

Both sentences have the same subject. The pronoun *we* in the second sentence takes the place of the compound subject *Ed and I.* Here we have two sentences which tell that the subjects did two different things.

You have already seen that compound predicates can be used to show that a subject is doing two different things. We can write a single sentence that has both a **compound subject** and a **compound predicate.**

Ed and I | **went** to the store and **bought** some spinach soup.

You can see the compound subject and compound predicate in this illustration:

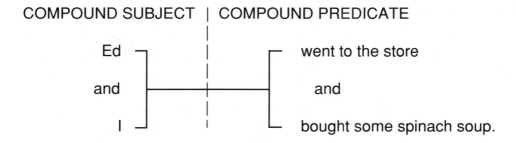

Always be sure that the parts of the compound subject belong together. Also be sure that the parts of the compound predicate belong together. When they do, you can write interesting sentences that combine all these parts into a single statement.

# ⬤ Simple Sentences and Compound Sentences

Look at these sentences. Each one makes a single statement.

> The bus | stopped at the corner. The passengers | got off.

A short line separates the subject from the predicate in each of these sentences. Each statement is a **simple sentence**.

---

- A **simple sentence** has *one subject* and *one predicate*.

---

Sometimes two simple sentences express thoughts that are related to each other. In the sentences about the bus, you know that the passengers got off *because* the bus stopped. These two ideas belong together.

When two simple sentences make statements that belong together, they can be connected so that the reader can see how they are related. We often use a word such as *and* to join two simple sentences.

> The bus stopped at the corner, **and** the passengers got off.

Now we have a **compound sentence**.

---

- A **compound sentence** joins two or more simple sentences. These simple sentences must express thoughts that clearly belong together.

---

- ## MAKING SURE THAT IDEAS BELONG TOGETHER

Here are two simple sentences. Do you think they should be joined to form a compound sentence?

It was raining very hard. My tuba was under the bed.

These two statements don't really have anything to do with each other, do they? The tuba could be under the bed even if the sun were shining. It would not make sense to join these two simple sentences into a compound sentence.

Do you think the next two sentences should be joined to form a compound sentence?

It was very windy. My hat blew off.

These two ideas *do* belong together, don't they? Your hat blew off *because* it was very windy. These two ideas should be combined into a compound sentence.

It was very windy, **and** my hat blew off.

If you are sure that two ideas belong together, then you can join them in a compound sentence. The compound sentence helps to show the reader *how* the thoughts are connected.

Our car wouldn't start. I was late for school.
Our car wouldn't start, **and** I was late for school.

**6**

- USING *AND* TO CONNECT PARTS OF A COMPOUND SENTENCE

In the compound sentences you just saw, the second part followed as a *result* of the first part. Here is how to write compound sentences that show the connection between two simple sentences:

---

- Remove the period at the end of the first simple sentence and use a *comma* (,) in its place. The *comma* shows that you are marking a slight break between two related parts of a compound sentence.

- Use the word *and* to show that the ideas in the two parts of the sentence belong together.

- Use only one capital letter at the beginning of the whole compound sentence.

---

Look at these pairs of simple sentences:

The dog barked. Then the cat ran away.

The students heard the bell. They all went to lunch.

The traffic light turned green. The cars began to move.

These pairs of sentences are related. You can make this clear to the reader by using *and* to write compound sentences.

The dog barked, **and** then the cat ran away.

The students heard the bell, **and** they all went to lunch.

The traffic light turned green, **and** the cars began to move.

## • USING *BUT* TO CONNECT PARTS OF A COMPOUND SENTENCE

Even though the word *and* is often used to join parts of a compound sentence, there are other words that can be used to write other kinds of compound sentences. How do you suppose these pairs of sentences might be connected?

It was cold and wet. I played baseball anyway.

Don wanted some cookies. He could find only carrots.

You would probably want to show the *contrast* between these pairs of simple sentences. This can be done by writing a compound sentence that uses the word *but* instead of *and* to show how the two parts are contrasted.

It was cold and wet, **but** I played baseball anyway.

Don wanted some cookies, **but** he could find only carrots.

## • USING *OR* TO CONNECT PARTS OF A COMPOUND SENTENCE

How are these pairs of simple sentences related to each other?

Do you want a pizza? Would you rather have spinach?

You can ride with us. You can take the bus.

These sentences offer a *choice*: Would you rather do this *or* that? Some of them ask questions, and some of them just tell us what the choices are. We can join these sentences with the word *or* in order to form compound sentences.

Do you want a pizza, **or** would you rather have liver?

You can ride with us, **or** you can take the bus.

## Predicate Adjectives

Adjectives are often used directly before the words they modify.

This is an **enormous** egg.

Sometimes adjectives are separated from the words they modify. When an adjective appears *after* the verb in the sentence, it is called a **predicate adjective**.

This egg is **enormous**.

---

- A **predicate adjective** is used after a linking verb to describe the subject of the sentence. The adjective is separated from the noun it modifies.

---

In the following examples, the first sentence of each pair uses an adjective just before a noun. The second sentence of each pair uses the same word as a predicate adjective.

We had a **terrible** storm. The storm was **terrible**.
A **yellow** light glowed in the sky. The light in the sky was **yellow**.

Predicate adjectives *must* be used when you want to describe a **pronoun**.

He was very **glad** to take a vacation.

We were **exhausted** after walking for two hours.

Remember that predicate adjectives are used only after linking verbs such as *is, are, was, were,* or *seem*.

## ● **Predicate Nouns**

Look at the words in boldface in these sentences.

My **cousin** is the best **swimmer** on the team.

The **mayor** of our town is a very good **speaker**.

All the boldface words are nouns. The first noun in each sentence is the subject. The other noun at the end of the sentence is called a **predicate noun**.

> • A **predicate noun** is used after a linking verb to tell what the subject of the sentence *is*.

Earlier you saw that the *predicate adjective* describes the subject by telling more about it. Now you see that the *predicate noun* gives more information that says what the subject *is*. This is another example of the importance of *linking verbs*. They connect information in the subject of the sentence with more information in the predicate.

In the next sentences the subject is a **pronoun**. You will see that the **predicate nouns** in boldface are used after linking verbs to refer to the subject of each sentence.

She is a famous **singer**.

They are all **friends** of mine.

We are **students** in the same class at school.

He was the best **pitcher** our team has ever had.

## Sentence Fragments

Is the following group of words as clear as it should be?

> I some fries and a hot dog.

You can see right away that this group of words does not say what the subject *did* with the fries and hot dog. You know that we must have a **verb** if this is going to be a real sentence.

> I **ate** some fries and a hot dog.

When a group of words does not make sense, it is often because it is a **sentence fragment**.

---

- A **sentence fragment** is only part of a sentence. Sentence fragments do not express complete thoughts. Fragments often lack either a subject or a verb.

---

What missing parts need to be added to these?

> My friend and I.

> Looking for four-leaf clovers.

The first example contains only a subject. In order to tell a complete thought, we must add a **predicate** that tells what my friend and I did. The second example could be the end of a sentence, but there is no **subject** to say who is looking for four-leaf clovers. The verb *are* could be used to join these two fragments into a complete sentence.

> My friend and I **are** looking for four-leaf clovers.

- CORRECTING SENTENCE FRAGMENTS

Look at another example. You should be able to find the **sentence fragment** here.

> My friend likes turtles. Are very slow.

The second group of words doesn't say *what* things are very slow. The first sentence started to talk about turtles, but *both* sentences must have subjects if they are going to make sense. It is easy to correct the sentence fragment by making this change.

> My friend likes turtles. **They** are very slow.

Now the plural pronoun *they* is the subject of the second sentence. This pronoun refers to the *turtles* mentioned in the first sentence.

Look at some more sentence fragments. In each one, we can't tell *who* did something or *what* they did because important words have been left out. Some of these fragments could come at the beginning of a sentence, and others could come at the end. None of these fragments will make sense until more words are added.

> And then they said.
>
> Are fun to play with.
>
> Carlos and Richard and I.
>
> Cheered at the end of the game.

Here we have added some words to complete these fragments.

> And then they said **they would be back before noon**.
>
> **My dogs** are fun to play with.
>
> Carlos and Richard and I **stayed until the movie ended**.
>
> **The whole crowd** cheered at the end of the game.

- CORRECTING SENTENCE FRAGMENTS (CONTINUED)

Sometimes sentences may not be clear because too many periods are used carelessly. These periods may break sentences into fragments. You can see this in the next example, which was written by a student your age.

> And my mom said. I have to go see this pool. and the man said. You can have the swimming pool.

If a sentence begins with "Mom said," then it must continue by telling us *what* she said. Here is how these sentence fragments can be corrected:

> My mom said, "I have to go see this pool." The man said, "You can have the swimming pool."

Just use a **comma** instead of a period after the word *said*, and use quotation marks (" ") to show that someone is speaking. We will look at quotation marks more closely in Chapter 7.

Sometimes it is possible to correct sentence fragments by using compound subjects or compound objects. Here is an example:

> I saw a lot of cars at the race. And a lot of people.

The second sentence is only a fragment, but this can be corrected by putting the two ideas together. The writer of these sentences saw two things: a lot of cars *and* a lot of people. We can combine all this into a single sentence.

> I | saw a lot of **cars and people** at the race.

You can see that the word *and* is very helpful when you want to join two or more things. You just have to be sure that they belong together.

# Run-on Sentences

It is important not to let sentences go on and on without any breaks at all. When this happens, we have **run-on sentences**.

> • **Run-on sentences** result when punctuation is omitted or is used incorrectly. Run-on sentences do not show that sentences should be separated because they express different thoughts.

• CORRECTING RUN-ON SENTENCES

Here is an example of a run-on sentence:

One day a boy got hurt his name is Todd he got hit by a baseball in the eye it is black and blue but it is going away.

Run-on sentences should be written as a group of separate sentences. Here is one way to correct the run-on sentence you just saw:

One day a boy got hurt. His name is Todd, and he got hit by a baseball in the eye. It is black and blue, but it is going away.

Now we have three sentences. They are clearer than the run-on sentence, but there is another way to make these sentences even better:

One day, a boy named Todd got hurt. He got hit in the eye by a baseball. His eye is black and blue, but it is getting better.

The important thing is to write separate sentences that have definite beginnings and endings. The writer must use clear punctuation so that the reader can understand each sentence.

## • CORRECTING RUN-ON SENTENCES (CONTINUED)

Look at these sentences written by students your age. The words are in the right order, but they are difficult to understand. Can you figure out what these sentences mean?

My dog is nice his name is Buster.

I like to play soccer in the spring it is fun.

They heard something loud it was a helicopter.

These are also run-on sentences that are difficult to understand. Each of these sentences has one subject and predicate near the beginning and *another* subject and predicate near the end. You can see this when we add a short line between the subjects and the verbs.

My **dog** | **is** nice his **name** | **is** Buster.

**I** | **like** to play soccer in the spring **it** | **is** fun.

**They** | **heard** something loud **it** | **was** a helicopter.

Now we will rewrite each example as two separate sentences. You can see that they are much easier to understand when these changes are made. Each sentence has its own subject and predicate, and each sentence begins with a **capital letter** and ends with a **period**.

My dog | is nice.  His name | is Buster.

I | like to play soccer in the spring.  It | is fun.

They | heard something loud.  It | was a helicopter.

- CORRECTING RUN-ON SENTENCES (CONTINUED)

Look at this story written by a student your age. You can see what happens when a run-on sentence just can't seem to stop.

**A Real Story**

One day I went to the park with my dog name Suzy and I like to play with her because she is nice and I was there with my Friend and they like to play with Suzy too and they like to make Suzy run so much that she gets tired and then she runs again and again so I like her too and she always goes to the window and don't let nobody go to the window and sometimes she sits on the window and then nobody can't go see out the window so I love Suzy very much and I like to kiss her face.

This whole story is one long sentence! The first thing to notice is that the word *and* is used over and over. Run-on sentences often use *and* instead of ending one sentence and beginning another one. If you find yourself using *and* over and over, you may be writing run-on sentences that need to be written as separate sentences.

Before we rewrite this example as several shorter sentences, let's look at some other mistakes that need to be corrected. At one point the writer says that Suzy "*don't* let *nobody* go to the window." This should be corrected to say that Suzy "*doesn't* let *anybody* go to the window."

The same thing happens when the writer says "*nobody can't* go see out the window." This should be written as "*nobody can* go see out the window."

Now let's write this story with clear sentences.

**6**

## • CORRECTING RUN-ON SENTENCES (CONTINUED)

Notice that we have removed some of the uses of *and*. Instead, we mark the end of each sentence with a period. Then we begin the next sentence by removing the word *and* and starting with a capital letter.

### A Real Story

One day I went to the park with my dog named Suzy. I like to play with her because she is nice. I was there with my friends. They like to play with Suzy, too. They like to make Suzy run so much that she gets tired, and then she runs again and again. I like her, too. She always goes to the window and doesn't let anybody go to the window. Sometimes she sits on the window and then nobody can see out of the window. I love Suzy very much, and I like to kiss her face.

We have used *and* only five times instead of the eleven times in the original version. Now the word *and* is used only to join things that belong together. None of the sentences begins with the word *and*.

# Using Verbs Correctly

- VERB TENSES

In Chapter 3 we looked at different **verb tenses**. When we talk about the **tense** of a verb, we are referring to *when* the action of the verb takes place. These are the verb tenses we have used so far:

**Present Tense:** The action of the verb takes place *now*.

> Today, the students **play** at recess.

**Past Tense:** The action of the verb took place in the *past*.

> Yesterday, the students **played** baseball.

**Future Tense:** The action of the verb will take place in the *future*.

> Tomorrow, the students **will play** basketball.

Now look at these sentences written by a student your age. Do you see anything unusual about the way the verbs are used?

> Yesterday we **went** to the lake. We **saw** a raccoon and **caught** lots of fish. Then we **eat** the fish and then we **went** home and **play** a game.

These sentences start to talk about something that happened *yesterday*. In the first two sentences, the verbs are in the past tense, as they should be (*went*, *saw*, and *caught*). Then the second sentence switches to the present tense (*eat*), back to the past tense (*went*), and then to the present tense again (*play*).

This is very confusing. The writer should use the past tense as long as he or she is telling about something that happened in the past. The tense of the verbs should not change at random, as it did in the example you just saw.

- ## MORE ABOUT VERB TENSES: FROM PAST TO FUTURE

If you do want to write about something in the past and then change to something that may happen in the future, you can make this clear to the reader.

> Last summer we **went** to the mountains. We **saw** lots of birds and animals. I **had** a lot of fun.
>
> Next summer we **will go** to the beach. We **will stay** there for a week. I know I **will have** lots of fun.

The first three sentences talk about what happened *last summer*. All the verbs are in the past tense. The last three sentences tell about things that will happen *next summer*. These verbs are all in the future tense. The sentences do not shift from one tense to another.

- ## AGREEMENT BETWEEN SUBJECT AND VERB

Here is another mistake to watch for:

> One of my friends are coming to see me.

The problem here is that the subject and the verb do not *agree* with each other. The subject is *one*, which is singular. It should be matched by the singular verb *is*. The word *friends* is plural, but it is *not* the subject and does not affect the verb.

> **One** of my friends **is** coming to see me.

Also be careful when a sentence begins with *there*.

> **There is** one more cookie left.

> **There are** three visitors to see you.

The first sentence uses the singular verb *is* because it is talking about *one* cookie. The second sentence uses the plural verb *are* because it is talking about *three* visitors.

**6**

# Using the Correct Pronoun as *Subject* or *Object*

In Chapter 2 you saw that pronouns can be used as the **subject** in a sentence. Pronouns may also be used as the **object** in a sentence. The following pairs of sentences show pronouns used first as the **subject** and then as the **object**.

**I** got a lot of presents for my birthday.
My brother gave a new baseball to **me**.

**They** are going to the mall.
I will go with **them**.

**We** waited for our friends to arrive.
They went with **us** to see a movie.

It is important to use the correct form of the pronoun in the **subject** part of the sentence. You must also be careful to use the **object** form of the pronoun in the *predicate*.

Here is a list to remind you which pronouns can be used as **subjects** and which can be used as **objects**. The *singular* and *plural* form for each set of pronouns is shown here.

| | SUBJECT PRONOUNS Singular | Plural | OBJECT PRONOUNS Singular | Plural |
|---|---|---|---|---|
| 1. | I | we | me | us |
| 2. | you | you | you | you |
| 3. | she | they | her | them |
| | he | | him | |
| | it | | it | |

On the next page you will see some of the problems that can appear when subject pronouns and object pronouns are used.

- SUBJECT PRONOUNS AND OBJECT PRONOUNS
  (CONTINUED)

Look at these sentences. Pronouns are used in the *subject* part of the sentence. Are these pronouns correct?

> **Me** and my friends play games.
>
> Sarah and **me** went to the park.
>
> **Him** and John played ball.

In the first sentence, you would not say "Me play games," would you? Then you wouldn't write the sentence this way. You also know that other people should be named before yourself in the sentence. If you check the list of pronouns, you see that *me* is an object pronoun, not a subject pronoun. The first sentence should be written this way:

> My friends and I play games.

The second sentence has the same problem. You wouldn't say "Me went to the park," so you wouldn't write the sentence this way. Here is the correct sentence:

> Sarah and I went to the park.

In the last sentence, you wouldn't say "Him played ball," would you? Here is the way this sentence should be written:

> **He** and John played ball.

## • SUBJECT PRONOUNS AND OBJECT PRONOUNS (CONTINUED)

Here is a sentence that uses pronouns as **objects**. See if these pronouns are correct.

> Dad gave some dandelions to **he** and **I**.

Again, check each pronoun by itself. If you look at the list of pronouns on page 153, you see that *he* and *I* are **not** object pronouns.

Would you say "Dad gave some apples to *he*"? Would you say he gave apples to *I*? No, you would say he gave apples to *him* and he gave apples to *me*. Here is the way the sentence should be written.

> Dad gave some dandelions to **him** and **me**.

---

When you have two words in the subject or two words in the object, check each one by itself to see if it is correct. Then you will be sure to use the right pronouns.

---

> John plays ball. I play ball.
> John and **I** play ball.

> They gave books to Ellen. They gave books to me.
> They gave books to Ellen and **me**.

**6**

ANSWERS BEGIN ON PAGE *248.*

## Sentence Fragments

*You may want to write answers on a separate piece of paper.*

1. Write **S** after the number if the **sentence** is complete. Write **F** after the number if it is only a **fragment**.

   1. a train trip through the mountains.

   2. Before they got here.

   3. Then I went through a haunted house.

   4. was the day I went to Florida.

   5. I have a little sister and two brothers.

2. Here are some sentence fragments. See if each fragment should come at the beginning or the end of a sentence. Then add enough words to make each sentence complete.

   1. It was very exciting when we.

   2. lets us go outside on nice days.

   3. Before school started.

   4. a very close friend to me.

   5. Each year on my summer vacation.

➡ *If you have trouble with any of these, talk to your parent or teacher.*

**6**

# CHECK YOUR UNDERSTANDING ✓

## Run-on Sentences

*You may want to write answers on a separate piece of paper.*

1. Write the letter **S** after the number of the examples that are simple sentences. Write the letter **R** for those examples that are **run-on sentences.**

    1. My friend is close to me she is my best friend.

    2. One of my favorite sports is golf.

    3. My two cats are both tabby cats they are very cute.

    4. My sister has dark brown hair.

    5. My eyes are blue I like to swim and ride bikes.

2. Make the corrections that will turn each example into two separate sentences.

    1. I have a dog I like him a lot.

    2. The storm started at night the power lines went out.

    3. There was a boy who liked video games he went to the arcade.

    4. I am nine years old I want to be a swimming teacher.

    5. My dog doesn't do anything he just eats and sleeps.

➡ *If you have trouble with any of these, talk to your parent or teacher.*

# 6

## ✓ CHECK YOUR UNDERSTANDING

### Verb Tenses

*You may want to write answers on a separate piece of paper.*

1. After each number write the **verb** that is used in each sentence. Also write *present*, *past*, or *future* to show the **tense** of the verb.

    1. We hurried to get out of the rain.

    2. Sometimes the ghost appears out of nowhere.

    3. The game will begin in half an hour.

    4. The wind blew a lot of leaves into our yard.

    5. We will carry some of these books for you.

2. The beginning of each sentence tells you *when* the sentence takes place. Use the correct **tense** of the verb in parentheses.

    1. Tomorrow I (go) to see my grandparents.

    2. Yesterday we (see) a good program on TV.

    3. Now he (try) to find the papers he misplaced.

    4. Last summer we (play) baseball almost every day.

    5. Next summer I (swim) a lot when we go to the beach.

3. In each of these examples the **verb tense** is wrong. Use the correct verb when you write each sentence on your paper.

    1. Last year my neighbor **has** an old dog named Ralph.

    2. Next week we **went** for a long drive.

    3. Yesterday I **watch** the storm blow the tree down.

    4. John **look** for his books for an hour last night.

    5. Tomorrow we **wash** all the windows.

➥ *If you have trouble with any of these, talk to your parent or teacher.*

# CHECK YOUR UNDERSTANDING ☑

## Using Subject Pronouns and Object Pronouns
*You may want to write answers on a separate piece of paper.*

**1.** Use the correct form of the pronouns in parentheses.

    1. Don said he saw Kevin and (I, me) yesterday.

    2. (We, us) are very good friends.

    3. I talked to Bill and (she, her) yesterday.

    4. (He, Him) and (I, me) are in the same class.

    5. I hope they will talk to (he, him) and (I, me).

**2.** Use one **pronoun** in place of each group of words in boldface. Here is an example:

        **Vera and Pam** are doing their homework.
        **They** are doing their homework.

    1. **Debbie** likes to ride horses.

    2. I saw **Andy and Dennis** riding their bikes.

    3. **My bike** needs some work on its brakes.

    4. **The dogs** were chasing their tails.

    5. **Russell and I** are on the same team.

**3.** In the second sentence of each pair, use a pronoun in the blank space. This pronoun should refer to the boldface words in the first sentence of each pair.

    1. **I** am working on math. My teacher helps ___.

    2. **Kim and Lisa** are friends. ____ like the same things.

    3. **Sally** is not here yet. See if you can find ___.

    4. **My skateboard** is broken. ___ needs a new wheel.

    5. **We** wanted some sandwiches. Mom made some for ___.

➥ *If you have trouble with any of these, talk to your parent or teacher.*

**6**

## ☑ *CHECK YOUR UNDERSTANDING*

## Compound Subjects, Objects, and Predicates

*You may want to write answers on a separate piece of paper.*

1. Combine each pair of sentences into a single sentence with a **compound subject**. Sometimes you will have to change the form of the verb. Here is an example:

> John **is** in my class. Ellen **is** in my class.
> John and Ellen **are** in my class.

1. Ann likes chocolate ice cream. I like chocolate ice cream.

2. Mary is a good student. Ross is a good student.

3. Jim played after school. Don played after school.

4. The dog is running. The squirrel is running.

5. Kim has freckles. Ted has freckles.

2. Combine each pair of sentences into a single sentence with a **compound object**. Here is an example:

> I waved to Tom. I waved to Debbie.
> I waved to Tom and Debbie.

1. Bo plays baseball. Bo plays football.

2. Joan likes to swim. Joan likes to ride horses.

3. We saw monkeys at the zoo. We saw tigers at the zoo.

4. You have a new bike. You have a new football.

5. She is good at math. She is good at spelling.

➥ *If you have trouble with any of these, talk to your parent or teacher.*

# CHECK YOUR UNDERSTANDING

## Compound Subjects, Objects, and Predicates
(continued)

*You may want to write answers on a separate piece of paper.*

**3.** Combine each pair of sentences into a single sentence with a **compound predicate**. Here is an example:

> Kate looked in her closet. Kate found her gloves.
> Kate looked in her closet and found her gloves.

1. I walked to the store. I bought some gum.

2. They raked the leaves. They cleaned the gutters.

3. Ann watched the sky. Ann saw the lightning flash.

4. The dog found my shoe. The dog chewed it to bits.

5. The car backed into the tree. The car dented its bumper.

➡ *If you have trouble with any of these, talk to your parent or teacher.*

**6**

☑ *Check Your Understanding*

## Simple and Compound Sentences

*You may want to write answers on a separate piece of paper.*

1. Write **simple** if the example is a simple sentence. Write **compound** if the example is a compound sentence.

   1. All my friends like to play basketball.

   2. We looked under the house, but we found it in the garage.

   3. Everybody seemed to enjoy the party.

   4. Giraffes are very large, and they have long necks.

   5. You can have chocolate cake, or you can have ice cream.

2. Here are some pairs of simple sentences. Rewrite each example so that it becomes a compound sentence. For these sentences, use the **comma** and the word ***and*** to join the two parts. Here is an example:

   > The snow fell all night.  It piled up against the house.
   > The snow fell all night, **and** it piled up against the house.

   1. We went to the park. We saw squirrels and chipmunks.

   2. They traveled all day. They finally got back home.

   3. I tried to solve the puzzle. I finally figured it out.

   4. The wind was blowing very hard. Several trees fell down.

   5. I had a birthday party. I asked my friends to come.

➡ *If you have trouble with any of these, talk to your parent or teacher.*

# CHECK YOUR UNDERSTANDING ☑

## Simple and Compound Sentences (continued)

*You may want to write answers on a separate piece of paper.*

3. Here are more pairs of simple sentences. These can be joined to form compound sentences, but they must be connected with the words *but* or *or* instead of *and*. Write each example as a compound sentence. Decide whether you should use *but* or *or* to join the two parts.

   1. I looked for an hour. I couldn't find anything.

   2. Do you want more spaghetti? Would you rather have broccoli?

   3. They thought they had the answer. They were mistaken.

   4. You can ride with us. You can take the bus.

   5. We worked hard all day. We didn't finish the job.

➡ *If you have trouble with any of these, talk to your parent or teacher.*

# PUNCTUATION
## Marks That Make the Sentence Clear

Is this a single sentence, or is it a group of sentences?

kim howard and pam went to the zoo they saw lions tigers and
elephants they also saw a lot of other animals birds and fish have
you ever been to the zoo i have

We can't tell when a sentence begins because there are no
capital letters. We can't tell when a sentence ends because
there are no periods or question marks or anything else.
Sometimes we can't even guess how the names of animals or
people are supposed to fit together. Is one of the children
named Kim Howard, or are there two children named Kim
and Howard? We can't tell.

In order to make sentences clear to the reader, we must
use certain marks to show how the words are organized.

> • **Punctuation marks** help the reader see how
> sentences are put together. They show the
> reader where sentences begin and end. They
> also show the reader how the words in each
> sentence are grouped together.

Now look again at the sentences that told about a trip to
the zoo. We have added **punctuation marks** to make the
sentences clear.

Kim, Howard, and Pam went to the zoo. They saw lions,
tigers, and elephants. They also saw a lot of other animals, birds,
and fish. Have you ever been to the zoo? I have.

**Punctuation Marks in the Sentence**

In Chapter 1 we talked about the marks that are used to show the beginning and end of every sentence. We will review those marks briefly here.

Every sentence begins with a **capital letter**. Also remember that every sentence must end with a punctuation mark which shows that the sentence is complete.

---

- The **period (.)** is used at the end of **declarative sentences**. These are sentences that make *statements*.

  Someone is knocking on the door.

---

- The **period** is also used at the end of **imperative sentences**. These are sentences that give *commands*. The subject is usually understood in imperative sentences.

  See who is at the door.

---

- The **question mark (?)** is used at the end of **interrogative sentences**. These are sentences that ask questions.

  Who was at the door?

---

- The **exclamation mark (!)** is used at the end of **exclamatory sentences**. These are sentences that make strong statements of feeling.

  I almost fainted when I saw who was at the door!

---

# ● Using Periods in Abbreviations

Although the period is used at the end of sentences that make statements and commands, it is also used in other important ways. Look at these sentences to see one of the ways the period can be used.

> Dr. Jones will arrive on Wednesday.
>
> Mrs. Evans will travel in November and December.
>
> Ms. Brown is talking to Mr. Whitney.

We could write out words such as *Doctor* and *Mister*, but we usually use **Dr.** and **Mr.** These are called **abbreviations**.

---

- An **abbreviation** is a shortened form of a word. In an abbreviation, some of the letters of the complete word are left out.
- Every abbreviation ends with a **period** to show that some letters have been omitted.

---

The abbreviations we just saw are the ones we use when we speak or write to someone we do not know very well. They are called **titles**, and they are used to help name a certain person. Titles are used especially when we write a letter to someone and when we address the envelope.

These are the titles that are used most often. Only the word *Miss* is never abbreviated.

> Ms.    Mrs.    Mr.    Dr.    Miss

## • MORE ABOUT ABBREVIATIONS

There is another way we use abbreviations when we write to someone and address an envelope. Here are some examples:

Mrs. Janice R. Edwards lives in Columbus, Ohio.

Mr. C. J. Green moved to Chicago.

Dr. Mary E. Franklin has an office on Main St.

He went from Syracuse, N.Y. to Raleigh, N.C.

Here we used only the first letter of some of the names of people and of the states *New York* and *North Carolina*. These letters are called **initials**. The word *initial* means "first." Initials can be used instead of writing out complete names of people or places.

---

- An **initial** is the first letter in the name of a person or place.
- An initial is always **capitalized** and ends with a **period**.

---

We often abbreviate other words when we address a letter. Here are some abbreviations and the words they stand for:

St. (Street)    Ave. (Avenue)    Rd. (Road)

These abbreviations also begin with a capital letter and end with a period. They are capitalized because they are part of a proper name. Here are some ways we can use these abbreviations:

Mr. Walters lives on First Ave. near my school.

Dr. Johnson has an office on Third St. near Scott Rd.

Mrs. Gomez lives on Elm St. near Walnut Ave.

Fargo, N.D., is a long way from Charleston, S.C.

## • OTHER ABBREVIATIONS

It is helpful to be able to abbreviate the names of the days of the week. Here is the way these abbreviations are written:

Mon. (Monday)　Tues. (Tuesday)　Wed. (Wednesday)

Thurs. (Thursday)　Fri. (Friday)　Sat. (Saturday)

Sun. (Sunday)

We can also abbreviate some of the names of the months. We do not abbreviate *May*, *June*, and *July* because these names are very short. The other months are abbreviated this way:

Jan. (January)　　Feb. (February)　　Mar. (March)

Apr. (April)　　　Aug. (August)　　Sept. (September)

Oct. (October)　　Nov. (November)　Dec. (December)

Remember that the names of the days and months are **proper nouns**. They always begin with capital letters. Every abbreviation must end with a period.

The names of states can be abbreviated. When the name of a state involves two words, we can use the initials:

N.Y. (New York)　　　N.M. (New Mexico)

N.D. (North Dakota)　S.D. (South Dakota)

N.C. (North Carolina)　S.C. (South Carolina)

Here are abbreviations for a few other states:

Penn. (Pennsylvania)　Calif. (California)

Mich. (Michigan)　　　Wisc. (Wisconsin)

Miss. (Mississipi)　　Mass. (Massachusetts)

## Using Commas

Are these sentences clear and easy to understand?

We spent April May and June in New York.

The movie was funny scary exciting.

Bill Allen Bob Dennis and I are friends.

These sentences are not very clear because several words of the same type are run together. We get lost when several adjectives or nouns are strung out in a row without any way to separate them.

The three sentences at the top of the page used several nouns or adjectives in a **series**. A *series* is a group of similar things that follow each other, one after another. When we write several nouns or adjectives in a series, we must use punctuation so that the reader can understand them.

The third sentence is especially confusing. Is it talking about two friends named *Bill Allen* and *Bob Dennis* or about four friends named *Bill*, *Allen*, *Bob*, and *Dennis*? In all these sentences, you can use the punctuation mark called the **comma** (,) to separate words and make the sentence clear.

We spent April, May, and June in New York.

The movie was funny, scary, and exciting.

Bill, Allen, Bob, Dennis, and I are friends.

---

- **Commas** (,) are used to separate similar words in a series. Usually these words will be nouns or adjectives. Sometimes they may be adverbs.
- Use a comma after each word in the series to separate it from the next one.
- Most of the time, a word such as *and* is used before the last word in the series.

---

## • COMMAS WITH WORDS IN A SERIES

Here are some more sentences that use commas. You can see that commas help to separate words that would be confusing if they all ran together.

He dressed up as a big, ugly, hairy monster.

Jane, Tom, and Sue are studying for the test.

The months of June, July, and August can be very hot.

The sunny, hot, humid weather was very uncomfortable.

So far we have seen some examples of how to use commas to separate words in a series. Let's review this important use of commas before we go on.

---

• **Use commas to separate *nouns* in a series.** Use a word such as *and* before the last noun in the series.

I saw **sheep, goats, and cows** on the farm.

**Alaska, Texas, and California** are large states.

---

• **Use commas to separate *adjectives* in a series.**

A **tiny, furry, frightened** rabbit ran across the yard.

Use a word such as *and* before the last adjective in the series when the adjectives appear in the *predicate*.

The weather was **cold, windy, and rainy**.

---

• **Use commas to separate *adverbs* in a series.** Use a word such as *and* before the last adverb in the series.

The deer ran **smoothly, swiftly, and quietly** through the forest.

The birds sang **sweetly, clearly, and loudly**.

---

# More Uses for Commas

- **Use a comma between the name of a *city* and a *state*.** Also use another comma after the *state* if the sentence is going to continue.

  I live in **Denver, Colorado**.

  I know someone in **Hartford, Connecticut**.

  They went to **Omaha, Nebraska**, and to **Phoenix, Arizona**.

---

- **Use a comma between the number of the *day* and the number of the *year* when you write the *date*.**

  Today is **October 23, 1989**.

  I was born on **March 14, 1980**.

  You may sometimes want to name the *day of the week* when you write the date. **Use another comma to separate the day of the week from the rest of the date.**

  Yesterday was **Monday, July 14, 1987**.

  Halloween comes on **Wednesday, October 31, 1990**.

---

- **Use a comma after the words *yes* or *no* at the beginning of a sentence.** Sometimes you may want to answer a question with a complete statement. This statement can begin with the words *yes* or *no*.

  Do you know where my coat is?  **Yes**, it is in the closet.

  Are they here yet?  **No**, I haven't seen them.

---

- MORE USES FOR COMMAS (CONTINUED)

---

- **Use a comma after the name of the person or group of people you are speaking to.**

    Sometimes you may want to use a **command** to ask a particular person or a group of people to do something. You can do this by naming the person at the beginning of the command. You may also want to ask a **question** of a particular person or group. When the sentence begins with the name of the person or the people being spoken to, use a **comma** after that name.

    > **Ellen,** please close the window when you leave.

    > **Class,** be sure to put the date on your papers.

    > **Students,** do you know who will visit us today?

    > **Maria,** can you give us the answer to this question?

---

- **Use a comma to separate the parts of a compound sentence.**

    In Chapter 6 you saw that two simple sentences can be combined to form a compound sentence.

    > Ed and Susan went to the zoo. They saw the baby panda.
    > Ed and Susan went to the zoo, **and** they saw the baby panda.

    When you write a compound sentence, always use the comma to separate the two parts. The comma is followed by a word such as *and* or *or* or *but*. Here are some more examples:

    > She looked through her telescope, **and** she finally saw the meteor.

    > We waited for an hour, **but** they never arrived.

    > They may come tomorrow, **or** they may wait until Saturday.

---

## • USING COMMAS IN SENTENCES

Here are some sentences taken from stories written for students your age. See how commas are used in each sentence.

> The pioneers raised their own food. Their main crops included wheat, corn, potatoes, fruits, and vegetables.
>
> Paul Bunyan had a light lunch of: 19 pounds of sausage, 6 hams, 8 loaves of bread, and 231 flapjacks.
>
> He packed a barrel of apples, honey and honeycombs, turnips and cabbage. When his cart was full, he waved good-bye to his wife, his daughter, and his son.
>
> She put knives, forks, and spoons at each place and set new tall candles in the center of the table. Later the table looked even more wonderful, piled high with steaming food—hot yellow corn bread, round bowls of green peas, roasted brown potatoes, a platter of cold venison, and golden pumpkin pies.

Here are a few more sentences written by students your age. These sentences also show how commas can be used.

> They got mops, brooms, rags, and a bucket.
>
> Her stories have excitement, fun, sad times, and good times.
>
> They built a fence so nobody would get hurt, but some boys climbed in anyway.
>
> To make a grilled cheese sandwich you need bread, cheese, butter, a pan, and a spatula.

# Quotation Marks

This is the beginning of a story about a talking mouse. It was written by a student your age. Can you tell when the mouse is actually talking?

> Tiger is a little mouse. I met him when I was walking. I just about stepped on him when he said, "Stop, don't step on me!" I looked down and saw a little tiny mouse. I said, "Who are you?" The little mouse looked up at me with fear and responded, "My name's Tiger." "Hello, Tiger," I said. "I won't hurt you. Jump up on my hand and you can walk with me."

You can easily see when the storyteller is speaking and when the mouse is speaking. This is because the spoken sentences have been written within **quotation marks.**

---

- **Quotation marks** ("  ") are used to show that someone is speaking.
- One quotation mark is used just *before* the first word that someone says. This word begins with a capital letter.
- Another quotation mark is used *after* the last spoken word.
- The last quotation mark usually comes *after* the punctuation mark that ends the spoken words.

---

Sometimes we begin by telling who is speaking, and then we tell what the person said.

> **He said,** "I can't find my books anywhere."

> **She said,** "I'll help you look for them."

A comma is used after the word *said*. Then the spoken part begins with a quotation mark and ends with another quotation mark after the period.

**7**

## • QUOTATION MARKS (CONTINUED)

We can also wait until the end of the sentence to tell who is speaking.

> "We don't have much more work to do," said Maria.

> "Let's hurry up and finish," said Robert.

Now the comma comes at the end of the spoken part and the quotation mark comes after the comma. Then we tell who is speaking and end the sentence with a period.

When you write sentences that make exclamations or ask questions, you use exclamation marks or question marks at the end of the spoken passage. Then you use quotation marks just as you used them in other sentences to show who is speaking.

> "When will we get there?" asked Tom.
> Sally exclaimed, "We'll *never* get there!"
> "Does anybody know where we are?" asked Mom.
> "I certainly hope so!" said Dad.

When one person speaks several sentences in a row, you don't need to set off every sentence with quotation marks. Use one mark at the beginning and another one when they have finished talking.

> Jamie said, "I have looked everywhere for my spelling book. I looked under the bed and under the house, and I even looked under the cat. I don't know where my book can be. Has *anybody* seen it?"
> "Maybe the dog ate it," said Mom.
> "No, I don't think so. He only likes arithmetic," replied Jamie.

# CHECK YOUR UNDERSTANDING
### ANSWERS BEGIN ON PAGE 256.

## Commas

*You may want to write answers on a separate piece of paper.*

1. Use commas to make these sentences clear to the reader. Also add periods where they are needed.

    1. We went to Chicago Illinois and to Detroit Michigan.

    2. The letter was sent on March 10 1990.

    3. They traveled to Idaho Montana and Utah on vacation.

    4. Today is Friday November 2 1990.

    5. I have friends in Buffalo N Y and in Santa Fe N M

2. Use commas as needed and add punctuation at the end of each sentence.

    1. Yes I know where he is

    2. John please tell your parrot to be quiet

    3. No she hasn't arrived yet

    4. Class we will be taking a trip tomorrow

    5. Joan will you see who is at the door

3. Use commas to separate the series of words in each sentence.

    1. Fred Ann and Tom were late for the bus.

    2. Washington Oregon and California are states in the west.

    3. My favorite pets are dogs cats frogs and elephants.

    4. The weather was mild pleasant and sunny.

    5. We saw roses daisies and marigolds in the flower garden.

➡ *If you have trouble with any of these, talk to your parent or teacher.*

**7**

## ☑ CHECK YOUR UNDERSTANDING

### Abbreviations and End Marks

*You may want to write answers on a separate piece of paper.*

1. Write each of these names correctly. Use capital letters and periods where they are needed.

    1. mr john edwards

    2. miss ellen white

    3. mrs alice franklin

    4. ms janice v adams

    5. mr allan b jones

    6. mrs a r williams

    7. dr thomas brown

    8. ms r ellen white

2. When you write these sentences, add capital letters for the first word and for all the proper nouns as well.

    1. bob and ellen are going to new york.

    2. mr and mrs elliott went home for thanksgiving.

    3. what costumes are sue and kim wearing for halloween?

    4. california is in the western united states.

    5. have you ever been to kansas or to iowa?

3. Write the *abbreviation* that matches each of the first four words. Then write the *word* that matches the last four abbreviations.

    1. Saturday ____

    2. February ____

    3. Wednesday ____

    4. October ____

    5. Sept. ____

    6. Jan. ____

    7. Mon. ____

    8. Dr. ____

➡ *If you have trouble with any of these, talk to your parent or teacher.*

# CHECK YOUR UNDERSTANDING ☑

## Abbreviations and End Marks (continued)

**4.** These sentences contain proper names and abbreviations that are not written correctly. The beginning and end of each sentence also need correction. Make the necessary changes when you write these sentences on your paper.

1. the letter was addressed to mr donald r jones in denver

2. i got back from houston and dallas in october

3. abraham lincoln was president during the civil war

4. did they say they were going to michigan or to minnesota

5. i first met mrs smith and ms jones in april of last year

➡ *If you have trouble with any of these, talk to your parent or teacher.*

**CHECK YOUR UNDERSTANDING**

## Quotation Marks

*You may want to write answers on a separate piece of paper.*

1.  Add the necessary quotation marks to show that someone is speaking in each of these sentences.

    1. He said, I will meet you at the movie this afternoon.

    2. Where has everyone gone? she asked.

    3. I don't know where they are, he said.

    4. Then she said, I will get there as soon as I can.

    5. I never saw such a big pumpkin! he exclaimed.

2.  Add quotation marks to show when someone is speaking. Also add commas as they are needed.

    1. They said We can't find our coats or umbrellas.

    2. How many cookies are left? she asked.

    3. John said We visited my aunt my cousin and my grandmother.

    4. What does your gorilla like to eat? asked Julie.

    5. Here are more cookies cakes and drinks said Mom.

➡ *If you have trouble with any of these, talk to your parent or teacher.*

# HANDBOOK FOR QUICK REFERENCE

## TABLE OF CONTENTS

## ADJECTIVES

- An **adjective** is a word that describes a noun.

Adjectives often tell what something *looks* like or *feels* like or *sounds* like. All the words for colors can be adjectives.

I have a **yellow** raincoat and **purple** boots.

The rabbit has **soft** fur. The **loud** noise frightened me.

Some adjectives tell *what kind* of thing or *how many* things you are talking about. All the words for *numbers* can be adjectives.

He ate **four** doughnuts and **two** pickles.

I saw a **big** bear at the zoo. There are **many** kinds of dogs and cats.

- THE ARTICLES *A, AN, THE*

The adjectives *a*, *an*, and *the* are called **articles**.

---

Use *a* and *an* to indicate *any* thing.
- Use *a* before a **singular noun** that begins with a **consonant**.

Do you have **a** cucumber I could borrow?

- Use *an* before a **singular noun** that begins with a **vowel**.

Has anyone found **an** orange umbrella?

---

Use *the* to indicate a *specific* thing or things. The article *the* is used before **singular *or* plural nouns**.

Did you see **the** beginning of **the** movie?

182

# Using Adjectives to Make Comparisons

Special endings must be added to adjectives when they are used to make comparisons.

- COMPARISONS USING *ER* AND *EST*

    Most of the time, the ending **er** is added to the adjective when only *two* things are compared. The ending **est** is added to the adjective when *more than two* things are compared.

    > Today is **colder** than yesterday was.

    > Monday was the **coldest** day we've had all winter.

    When the adjective ends with *two consonants*, add **er** and **est** without changing the spelling of the adjective.

    > fast, faster, fastest    long, longer, longest

    When the adjective ends with one vowel and one consonant, double the final consonant before adding **er** and **est.**

    > hot, hotter, hottest    big, bigger, biggest

    When the adjective ends with the letter **e**, drop this **e** before adding **er** and **est.**

    > nice, nicer, nicest    brave, braver, bravest

    When the adjective ends with **y**, this **y** must be changed to **i** before you add **er** and **est.**

    > pretty, prettier, prettiest    heavy, heavier, heaviest

- COMPARISONS USING *GOOD* AND *BAD*

  The adjectives *good* and *bad* do not add **er** and **est**. These adjectives have special spellings when they are used to compare things.

  > good, better, best        bad, worse, worst

- COMPARISONS USING *MORE* AND *MOST, LESS,* AND *LEAST*

  Many adjectives that contain *more than one syllable* cannot simply add **er** and **est.** These adjectives must be combined with other words in order to make comparisons.

  ---

  The words ***more*** and ***most*** are used to show larger and larger amounts or degrees.

  > beautiful, more beautiful, most beautiful
  >
  > exciting, more exciting, most exciting

  ---

  The words ***less*** and ***least*** show smaller and smaller amounts or degrees.

  > difficult, less difficult, least difficult
  >
  > famous, less famous, least famous

  ---

- USING ADJECTIVES IN THE SENTENCE.

  Adjectives are often placed just before the nouns they describe, but they can also be used in the predicate of the sentence after a *linking verb*. These adjectives are separated from the nouns they modify.

  > The **heavy** rainstorm lasted for hours.
  > The rainstorm was very **heavy**.

## ADVERBS

> • An **adverb** is a word that can be used to tell more about a **verb**.

Many adverbs tell *how* something happened or *when* it happened or *where* it happened.

The car rolled **slowly** to a stop.

We walked **quickly** through the wind and snow.

I **always** play ball at recess.

**Sometimes** we visit my grandparents.

Look **up** in the attic for the snow shovel.

The ball rolled over **there** under the bush.

• ADVERBS ENDING WITH *-LY*

Many times, an adjective can be changed to an adverb by adding the letters *-ly* to the adjective.

quiet, quiet**ly**     safe, safe**ly**

slow, slow**ly**     quick, quick**ly**

This is **quiet** music. The music played **quietly**.

It was a **safe** journey. They arrived **safely** back home.

Some adjectives already end with *y*. Change this *y* to *i* before adding *-ly* when you use these words as adverbs.

happy, happily     easy, easily     noisy, noisily

## ANTONYMS

- **Antonyms** are words that mean the opposite of each other.

Here are a few antonyms you often use.

| | | |
|---|---|---|
| up, down | in, out | before, after |
| fast, slow | day, night | inside, outside |
| big, little | hot, cold | strong, weak |
| soft, hard | wet, dry | tall, short |

In the following sentences, the antonyms are *adverbs* that tell more about the verb of each sentence.

> Look **up** in the attic for your boots. Then look **down** in the basement for them.

> The cat is **inside**, next to the fire. The dog is **outside**, playing in the mud.

In the next sentences, the antonyms are *adjectives* that tell more about nouns.

> Evan has a very **big** dog, but I have a very **little** one.

> Today it is very **hot**, but yesterday it was **cold**.

## COMPOUND WORDS

- A **compound word** is made up of two or more separate words joined together.

Often you can tell the meaning of the compound word if you know the meaning of the words that have been combined. Many compound words are written with no break between the two individual words. These are called **closed compounds**.

| | |
|---|---|
| football | sunburn |
| baseball | cheerleader |
| basketball | sunshine |
| classroom | skateboard |
| chalkboard | birthday |
| playground | notebook |
| sidewalk | raincoat |
| airplane | homework |

Some compound words are joined by a short line called a *hyphen* (-). This hyphen shows that the words belong together. These are called **hyphenated compounds**.

| | |
|---|---|
| baby-sitter | hide-and-seek |
| go-cart | merry-go-round |
| ice-skate | grown-ups |

A few compound words are not joined together. You know that these pairs of words belong together and have a meaning that is different from the meaning of each word alone. These are called **open compounds**.

| | |
|---|---|
| no one | all right |
| hot dog | ice cream |
| guinea pig | roller coaster |

## CONTRACTIONS

- A **contraction** is made up of two words combined into one. At least one letter in one of the words is left out. An **apostrophe (')** takes the place of the missing letter.

Many contractions involve a verb followed by the word *not*. Other contractions combine a pronoun with a shortened form of a verb.

- CONTRACTIONS WITH A VERB AND *NOT*

When the word *not* follows a verb in a contraction, use an **apostrophe (')** to take the place of the *o* in *not*.

Here are some contractions you often use.

| | |
|---|---|
| don't (do not) | doesn't (does not) |
| didn't (did not) | won't (will not) |
| isn't (is not) | aren't (are not) |
| wasn't (was not) | weren't (were not) |
| haven't (have not) | hasn't (has not) |
| hadn't (had not) | couldn't (could not) |
| wouldn't (would not) | shouldn't (should not) |

- CONTRACTIONS WITH PRONOUNS AND A VERB

When a pronoun is followed by a verb in a contraction, use an **apostrophe (')** to take the place of the omitted letters in the verb.

Here you see contractions that combine pronouns with the important irregular verbs *be* and *have* in the present tense.

| | |
|---|---|
| I'm (I am) | we're (we are) |
| you're (you are) | he's (he is) |
| she's (she is) | it's (it is) |
| they're (they are) | |

| | |
|---|---|
| I've (I have) | we've (we have) |
| you've (you have) | they've (they have) |
| he's (he has) | she's (she has) |
| it's (it has) | |

The contraction *he's* can stand for *he is* or *he has*. The contraction *she's* can stand for *she is* or *she has*, and *it's* can stand for *it is* or *it has*. You can tell which meaning is used if you look at the whole sentence.

**It's** very cold today. (**It is** very cold today.)

**It's** been cold for a week. (**It has** been cold for a week.)

The verb *will* can also be combined with pronouns.

| | |
|---|---|
| I'll (I will) | we'll (we will) |
| you'll (you will) | they'll (they will) |
| he'll (he will) | she'll (she will) |
| it'll (it will) | |

Remember to use the apostrophe in every contraction. This is the only way to show the difference between words such as *well* and *shell* and contractions such as *we'll* and *she'll*.

Be careful to notice the difference between contractions and those words that have the same sound.

**It's** is a contraction of **it is**.

> **It's** raining now.

**Its** is a possessive pronoun.

> The school is proud of **its** team.

---

**You're** is a contraction of **you are**.

> **You're** going to like this a lot.

**Your** is a possessive pronoun.

> Have you found **your** missing suspenders?

---

**They're** is a contraction of **they are**.

> **They're** leaving in an hour.

**Their** is a possessive pronoun.

> My friends are looking for **their** dog.

**There** is often used as an adverb.

> Your hamster is **there** under the chair.

Remember to use the apostrophe in the contraction *let's.* This is a shortened form of the words *let us.*

## HOMOPHONES

- **Homophones** are words that have the *same sound* but *different spellings* and *different meanings*.

Here are some pairs of homophones. Be careful to write the word that has the meaning you want.

| | | |
|---|---|---|
| I, eye | for, four | ate, eight |
| no, know | one, won | peace, piece |
| new, knew | be, bee | right, write |
| its, it's | by, buy | wood, would |
| see, sea | blue, blew | flour, flower |
| hole, whole | here, hear | threw, through |

Sometimes you find groups of *three* words that have the same sound but different spellings. Be very careful to use the correct word in your sentences. Here are two groups of homophones you use very often.

to, too, two      there, their, they're

Notice that the word *they're* is a **contraction**. This contraction is made up of the words *they are*. An **apostrophe** is used to take the place of the missing letters. These sentences show how to use these homophones.

I walked **to** the store. My little brother came, **too**.
We bought **two** candy bars.

**There** is my book. I saw **their** books on the table.
**They're** coming to get them soon.

## NOUNS

- A **noun** is a word that names a *person*, a *place*, or a *thing*.

Many nouns are **base words** that make sense all by themselves. Base words show how the word is spelled before endings are added.

## ● Singular Nouns

Singular nouns name only *one* person, place, or thing.

| | | | |
|---|---|---|---|
| PERSON: | boy | girl | friend |
| PLACE: | school | town | museum |
| THING: | book | car | pencil |

## ● Plural Nouns

Plural nouns name *more than one* person, place, or thing. Special endings must be added to base words in order to change singular nouns to plural nouns.

- ADDING *S* AND *ES*

Add **s** to form the plural of most nouns.

| | | | |
|---|---|---|---|
| PEOPLE: | boy**s** | girl**s** | friend**s** |
| PLACES: | school**s** | town**s** | museum**s** |
| THINGS: | book**s** | car**s** | pencil**s** |

Add *es* to form the plural of nouns that end with the letters *s* or *ss*, *x*, *ch*, and *sh*.

| | | |
|---|---|---|
| bus, bus**es** | glass, glass**es** | address, address**es** |
| box, box**es** | watch, watch**es** | bush, bush**es** |

192

# More about Plural Nouns

- ## NOUNS ENDING WITH *Y*

Many nouns end with a *consonant* followed by the letter *y*. To write the plural form of these nouns, *change the y to i and add es*.

| | | |
|---|---|---|
| sky, sk**ies** | baby, bab**ies** | bunny, bunn**ies** |
| lady, lad**ies** | story, stor**ies** | family, famil**ies** |

Some nouns end with a *vowel* followed by the letter *y*. To write the plural form of these nouns, *just add the letter s*. Also add *s* to nouns that end with *ie*.

| | | |
|---|---|---|
| boy, boy**s** | day, day**s** | key, key**s** |
| pie, pie**s** | movie, movie**s** | chimney, chimney**s** |

- ## NOUNS ENDING WITH *O*

Nouns that end with a *vowel* and *o* add only the letter *s* to form the plural.

radio, radio**s**   video, video**s**   rodeo, rodeo**s**

Most nouns that end with a *consonant* and *o* add *es* to form the plural.

tomato, tomato**es**   volcano, volcano**es**   hero, hero**es**

- ## IRREGULAR PLURAL NOUNS

A few nouns *do not* add *s* or *es* to form the plural. These nouns have irregular plural forms:

| | | |
|---|---|---|
| man, men | woman, women | child, children |
| person, people | foot, feet | tooth, teeth |
| mouse, mice | goose, geese | ox, oxen |

## Common Nouns and Proper Nouns

**Common nouns** name *any* person, place, or thing.

| | | | | | |
|---|---|---|---|---|---|
| PERSON: | boy | girl | friend | mother | father |
| PLACE: | house | school | building | city | country |
| THING: | book | car | shoe | table | pencil |

**Proper nouns** name *specific* people, places, or things.
**Proper nouns always begin with *capital letters*.**

| | | |
|---|---|---|
| PERSON: | George Washington | Abraham Lincoln |
| PLACE: | Chicago | United States |
| THING: | Statue of Liberty | Washington Monument |

All the names of people are proper nouns. The names of your family and friends are proper nouns. The names of cities and states and countries are proper nouns. All these words should begin with capital letters.

All the names of the **days of the week** are proper nouns.

Sunday   Monday   Tuesday   Wednesday   Thursday  Friday
Saturday

All the names of the **months** are proper nouns.

| | | | |
|---|---|---|---|
| January | February | March | April |
| May | June | July | August |
| September | October | November | December |

# Possessive Nouns

**Possessive nouns** are used when you want to show that something *belongs to* someone. Possessive nouns require special marks added to the base word.

- SINGULAR POSSESSIVE NOUNS

 To write a singular possessive noun, add an **apostrophe** and the letter *s* (*'s*) to the end of the singular noun.

 Where is the **dog's** collar? This is my **teacher's** desk.

- PLURAL POSSESSIVE NOUNS

When you write the plural possessive form of a noun, first write the regular plural noun. Then add an **apostrophe** if the plural noun ends with the letter *s.*

 These are the **boys'** books. Here are my **friends'** coats.

When the plural noun does *not* end with *s,* then add an **apostrophe** and *s* (*'s)* to the end of the plural form.

 Those are the **women's** umbrellas.

 Where are the **children's** pet kangaroos?

These guidelines will help you remember how to write possessive nouns:

---

Add an **apostrophe** and *s* (*'s*) to any noun that does not already end with *s* or *es.*

Add only an **apostrophe** (*'*) to any noun that does end with *s* or *es.*

---

## PREFIXES

- A **prefix** is a word part that is added to the *beginning* of a *base word*.

A *base word* is a complete word that makes sense all by itself. It has no endings added or other changes in spelling.

A **prefix** is *not* a complete word, but it does change the meaning of the base word. Here are some prefixes you often use:

*un-* means "not" or "the opposite of something."

*dis-* also means "not" or "the opposite of something."

*re-* means "again" or "back."

These sentences use words that begin with the three prefixes you just saw.

Will this key **unlock** the door?

I **disagree** with the things he said.

It is important to **recycle** paper and plastic.

This carrot has an **unusual** flavor.

Do you **dislike** the taste of pickles?

I must **repay** the money I borrowed.

## PRONOUNS

- A **pronoun** is a word that takes the place of a noun.

Kim is in my class. **She** is my best friend.

A pronoun can be used as the *subject* of a sentence or as an *object* in a sentence.

## ● Subject Pronouns

Each of these pronouns can be used as the **subject** of the sentence:

| SUBJECT PRONOUNS | | |
|---|---|---|
| | **Singular** | **Plural** |
| 1. | I | we |
| 2. | you | you |
| 3. | he | they |
| | she | |
| | it | |

The following sentences use subject pronouns:

**I** like to swim with my friends.

**We** went to the zoo yesterday.

**You** will like this ice cream.

**He** is looking for his missing tadpole.

**She** and **I** are friends.

**They** are next door playing with their pet shark.

 **Object Pronouns**

Pronouns can also be used as *objects* in the predicate part of the sentence. These pronouns come *after* the verb and tell who or what receives the action of the verb.

| OBJECT PRONOUNS | |
|---|---|
| **Singular** | **Plural** |
| 1. me | us |
| 2. you | you |
| 3. him | them |
| her | |
| it | |

Here are some sentences that use object pronouns:

They gave some cookies to **me.**

John and Harriet saw **us** at the movie.

Please give these pencils to **him** and to **her.**

We will meet **them** at the restaurant.

---

When you write about yourself and someone else, always put the other person's name first. This is true when you use **subject pronouns** and when you use **object pronouns.**

**Ellen and I** wanted some doughnuts. (Subject)
Mom gave some doughnuts to **Ellen and me**. (Object)

**He and I** were walking in the rain. (Subject)
A car splashed water on **him and me.** (Object)

---

## ● Possessive Pronouns

**Possessive pronouns** are used to show that something *belongs* to someone. These pronouns are always followed by a noun.

| POSSESSIVE PRONOUNS | |
| --- | --- |
| **Singular** | **Plural** |
| 1.  my | our |
| 2.  your | your |
| 3.  his | their |
| her | |
| its | |

These sentences use possessive pronouns:

I don't know where I left **my** books.

Our dog likes to chew on **our** shoes.

Your bike is next to **their** house.

He found **his** hamster under the couch.

**Her** papers fell on the floor.

The car stopped when **its** tire went flat.

## PUNCTUATION

- **Punctuation** refers to the marks we use to make our sentences clear to the reader. Some *punctuation marks* show where sentences begin and end. Other marks show how groups of words are organized within the sentence.

## Punctuating Sentences

Every sentence begins with a **capital letter.** Each sentence must also end with a **punctuation mark** which shows the reader that the sentence is complete.

---

A **period (.)** is used at the end of a **declarative sentence** and an **imperative sentence.**

> They lived happily ever after.

> Close the door when you leave.

---

A **question mark (?)** is used at the end of an **interrogative sentence.**

> Is this the book you wanted?

---

An **exclamation mark (!)** is used at the end of an **exclamatory sentence.**

> That was a fantastic ball game!

---

# ● Commas

A **comma (,)** is used to separate words in a series. A *series* is a group of similar things that follow one after the other. When several similar words are used in a series, they should be separated so the reader can understand them. Often the word *and* is used before the last word in the series.

> My pet monster is big, lazy, bashful, and green.

> I saw lions, tigers, monkeys, and elephants.

> A small, slow, frightened turtle hid in the bushes.

Use a comma between the name of a **city** and a **state.**

> My friend moved to Denver, Colorado.

Use a comma between the **day** and the **year** when you write the date.

> He was born on October 23, 1980.

Use a comma after the words *yes* and *no* when they begin a sentence.

> Yes, I know where he is.

> No, I don't know when he will be back.

Use a comma after the name of the person who is spoken to. This will often happen at the beginning of a sentence.

> Maria, will you help me do the dishes?

Use a comma after the **greeting** and the **closing** in a letter.

> Dear Mr. Jones,     Dear Mrs. Evans,

> Sincerely,             Yours truly,

# Apostrophes

The **apostrophe (')** is used in two important ways.

> • An **apostrophe** is used to form **possessive nouns.** These nouns show that something belongs to someone.

Add an **apostrophe** and the letter *s ('s)* to singular nouns and to those plural nouns that do not already end with *s.*

| | | |
|---|---|---|
| The girl's book | The boy's shoe | John's hat |
| Mary's dog | The men's cars | The children's coats |

Add *only* an apostrophe to nouns that already end with *s.*

Two dogs' collars          Three cats' toys

> • The **apostrophe** is used in **contractions** to show that letters have been left out of a word.

| | | |
|---|---|---|
| I am - I'm | she will - she'll | you are - you're |
| he is - he's | I do not - I don't | they cannot - they can't |

# Quotation Marks

**Quotation marks (" ")** are used to show that someone is speaking. These marks are used at the *beginning* and the *end* of the words that are spoken.

Mary said, "I don't know where my dog is."
Lisa said, "I saw him in the backyard."
"Let's go see if he's still there!" said Mary.

# Capitalization

Use a capital letter at the beginning of every sentence.

**H**ere is one of the socks I lost. **W**here is the other one?

Capitalize all **proper nouns.** These are the names of specific people, places, or things. Remember that the names of days and months are *proper nouns.*

**A**braham **L**incoln   **C**hicago, **I**llinois   **A**tlantic **O**cean

**M**onday   **F**riday   **M**arch   **D**ecember

# Periods in Abbreviations

The **period (.)** is used to show that letters have been left out of a word. These shortened words are called **abbreviations.**

Mr. (Mister)      Dr. (Doctor)      St. (Street)

Ave. (Avenue)     Mon. (Monday)     Feb. (February)

A period is also used with **initials.** An initial is the first letter in the name of a person or place. It is always capitalized.

Mr. J. L. Evans lives in Princeton, N.J.

# The Colon

A **colon (:)** is used between the hour and the minute when you write the time. Use **a.m.** to show that it is morning and **p.m.** to show that it is afternoon or evening. These letters are also abbreviations and must end with a period.

It is now 11:15 a.m. The game begins at 1:30 p.m.

## SENTENCES

- A **sentence** is a group of words that expresses a complete thought. It tells who or what is doing something, and it tells what they are doing.

Maria walked to school yesterday.

My friends and I like to play baseball and soccer.

Every sentence contains a **subject** and a **predicate.**

 # The Subject of the Sentence

- The **subject** is the part of the sentence that tells who or what is doing something. It tells what the sentence is about.

The **complete subject** includes all the words in the subject part of the sentence. In the following sentences, the complete subject includes all the words that come *before* the short line.

My school | is not far from my home.

Fred's dog | is big and lazy.

My parents and I | went to see my grandmother.

The **simple subject** tells *exactly* who or what is doing something. Here the simple subject is printed in boldface.

My new **bike** | is fun to ride.

Ellen's favorite **snake** | is under the table.

My **friend** | got caught in the rain.

# The Predicate of the Sentence

- The **predicate** is the part of the sentence that tells what the subject *does* or what it *is*. The predicate completes the meaning of the sentence.

The **complete predicate** contains *all* the words that tell what the subject is or is doing. In the following sentences, the complete predicate includes all the words that come *after* the short line.

> They | played baseball for an hour.

> Last night, I | saw the full moon.

> Everybody in my class | went on a field trip.

The **simple predicate** is the word or words that tell exactly what the subject is doing. The simple subject is usually the *verb*. In the following sentences, the simple *predicate* is printed in boldface.

> That night he | **heard** a noise in the attic.

> The ghost | **bumped** down the stairs.

> He | **will return** when the weather is better.

> Most of the people | **believe** the story.

## Types of Sentences

There are four types of sentences. No matter what type of sentence you write, remember that **every sentence begins with a capital letter.**

- **Declarative sentences** make statements. A **period (.)** marks the end of each declarative sentence.

    I like living on a farm.

    Once there was a dragon who was sort of nice.

- **Interrogative sentences** ask questions. A **question mark (?)** is used at the end of each interrogative sentence.

    Who took my peanut butter sandwich?

    Did you see what happened?

- **Imperative sentences** give instructions or ask someone to do something. In imperative sentences, the subject is usually understood and is not written out. This is because the command or the request is addressed directly to someone. A **period (.)** marks the end of each imperative sentence.

    Look for a street sign.

    Please ask someone for directions.

- **Exclamatory statements** make strong statements of feeling. The **exclamation mark (!)** is used at the end of each exclamatory sentence.

    That was a fantastic movie!

    I was amazed when I heard the news!

## SUFFIXES

- A **suffix** is a word part that is added to the *end* of a *base word*.

A **base word** is a complete word that makes sense all by itself. It has had no endings added or other changes made.

A **suffix** is not a complete word, but it does help to create a new word that is related to the meaning of the base word. Here are some suffixes you use very often.

*-er* can be used to show *who* or *what* is doing something. This suffix often changes a verb to a noun. Here are some verbs that are changed to nouns by adding the suffix *-er* to a base word.

| VERB | NOUN |
|---|---|
| run | runner |
| play | player |
| write | writer |
| win | winner |
| teach | teacher |
| help | helper |
| swim | swimmer |

When the base word ends with a single vowel and a single consonant, double the final consonant before adding *-er* (*swim, swimmer*).

*-or* can also be used to show who or what is doing something. This suffix is not always added to a verb, but it does name the person who is doing something.

| | | |
|---|---|---|
| actor | mayor | author |
| doctor | director | inventor |
| sailor | visitor | supervisor |

*-ly* means "in a certain way" or "to a certain extent." This suffix is often used to change an *adjective* to an *adverb.* Here are some adjectives that are changed to adverbs by adding the suffix *-ly.*

| Adjective | Adverb |
| --- | --- |
| quick | quickly |
| quiet | quietly |
| slow | slowly |
| sudden | suddenly |
| most | mostly |
| exact | exactly |

*-ful* means "filled with" or "having the qualities of something." This suffix is used to form **adjectives** that tell more about a noun. Notice that the suffix *-ful* is spelled with one *l.* Here are some sentences that show how to use words ending with the suffix *-ful.*

These leaves have bright **colors.** They are very **colorful.**

Maria and I will **help** wash the car. We will be very **helpful.**

*-less* means "without" or "not having something." This suffix also forms **adjectives** when you add it to a word. Here are some sentences showing how to use the suffix *-less.*

They did not take **care** when they were washing the dishes. They broke some because they were **careless.**

We didn't have any **hope** that we could win the game. We thought it was **hopeless.**

## SYNONYMS

- **Synonyms** are words that mean almost the same thing.

Here are a few familiar synonyms.

small, little, tiny

big, large, huge

fast, swift, speedy

tired, sleepy

begin, start

end, finish

gift, present

bright, shiny, brilliant

Synonyms allow you to vary your sentences and avoid using the same words over and over. The following sentences show how synonyms can be used. Two or three words are shown in parentheses. You can choose the word that best expresses the meaning you want.

I hoped I would get lots of (gifts, presents) for my birthday.

When did you (begin, start) to paint the house?

I saw a (bright, shiny, brilliant) light across the lake.

We were very (tired, sleepy) after the long trip.

## VERBS

- A **verb** is a word that expresses an *action* or that tells what something *is*. The verb is the most important word in the **predicate** of the sentence.

In these sentences the verbs are printed in boldface:

Maria and I **are** in the same class.

We **played** football in the yard.

My dog **runs** around and **barks** at everything.

## Action Verbs and Linking Verbs

- Many verbs tell what the subject of the sentence is *doing*. These are called **action verbs.**

I **hit** the ball as hard as I could.

The storm **blew** several trees down.

We **rode** our bikes all over the place.

- Other verbs do not express actions, but they do tell what the subject of the sentence *is*. These are **linking verbs** which connect the subject with additional information in the predicate.

I **am** in the third grade at school.

My pet gorilla **is** very smart.

Both his parents **are** doctors.

The wind **seems** much weaker now.

# Verb Tenses

- The **tense** of a verb tells *when* the action happened.

The three most important tenses are the **present,** the **past,** and the **future.**

PRESENT TENSE

- The **present tense** is used to tell about things that are happening right now or that happen over and over.

The *base form* of the verb is used with most subjects in the present tense. The base form of a verb shows the spelling of the word before endings are added.

> I **play** baseball whenever it isn't raining.

With some subjects, we must add endings to verbs in the present tense.

The letter *s* is added to the base form of most verbs when the subject is *he, she, it,* or a singular noun.

> My sister **helps** me with my homework.

> She **shows** me how to correct my mistakes.

> My brother **likes** math and science.

The letters *es* are added to verbs that end with *ss, x, sh,* or *ch* when the subject is *he, she, it*, or a singular noun.

> Dad **washes** the car every Saturday.

> My dog **misses** his favorite bone.

> I hope mom **fixes** my broken chopsticks.

## PAST TENSE

- The **past tense** is used to tell about things that have already happened. Most of the time the letters *ed* are added to the base form of a verb to show the past tense.

Yesterday we **watched** a movie on TV.

Last week I **played** soccer with my friends.

Last summer my family **traveled** to California.

Verbs that add *ed* in the past tense are called *regular verbs*.

When a verb ends with a consonant and the letter *y,* then the *y* must be changed to *i* before *ed* is added.

I **carried** all the boxes into the attic yesterday.

When the verb ends with *e,* drop this *e* before adding *ed*.

We **waved** good-bye as our friends got on the train.

## FUTURE TENSE

- The **future tense** tells about things that *will happen.* To write the future tense, just add the word *will* before the base form of the verb.

We **will go** to Disneyland next summer.

Mike and Dennis **will meet** us at the mall this afternoon.

I **will show** them my new gerbil tomorrow.

# Main Verbs and Helping Vers

---

- **Main verbs** tell exactly what the subject *is* or what it is *doing*.

---

My pet skunk **is** fun to play with.

His friends **are** all on the baseball team.

I **play** football every Saturday.

My brother **plays** for his school team.

---

- **Helping verbs** are used to assist main verbs. They help to express actions or make statements. Helping verbs always come *before* main verbs.

---

In the future tense, the helping verb *will* is used before the base form of the main verb.

We **will play** a game next Saturday.

There are other helping verbs that are often combined with main verbs. Here are some sentences that use a helping verb before a main verb:

I **have seen** that movie three times.

He **has gone** to the store for some mustard.

They **had worked** on the road for two days

My friends **are going** to Disneyland.

Some people **were waiting** in line for the movie.

Some of the most important helping verbs are *have*, *has*, and *had*. On pages 215–216 you will see that some main verbs have special spellings when they are combined with these helping verbs.

# Irregular Verbs

**Irregular verbs** do not follow the patterns you have just seen. These verbs do not simply add *ed* in the past tense, and they may have unusual spellings in other tenses as well.

## • THE VERB *BE*

One of the most important irregular verbs is **be.** This verb does not add *s* after *he* or *she* and does not add *ed* to form the past tense. In fact, the base form *be* is not even used in the present tense or the past tense.

| **PRESENT TENSE** | | **PAST TENSE** | |
| **Singular** | **Plural** | **Singular** | **Plural** |
| 1. I am | we are | I was | we were |
| 2. you are | you are | you were | you were |
| 3. he is | they are | he was | they were |
| she is | | she was | |
| it is | | it was | |

In the future tense the base form *be* is combined with the helping verb *will* for all subjects, singular and plural.

I **will be** in the school play next week.

We **will be** in Hoboken on Saturday.

On page 210 you saw that the verb *be* is one of the most important **linking verbs.** It connects information in the subject with additional information in the predicate.

I **am** in the third grade.

Carlos **is** my friend.

The weather **is** very hot.

My neighbors **are** away on vacation.

# More about Irregular Verbs

## • THE VERB *HAVE*

Another irregular verb is *have*. Here is how it is written in the present tense and the past tense:

| PRESENT TENSE | | PAST TENSE | |
|---|---|---|---|
| **Singular** | **Plural** | **Singular** | **Plural** |
| 1. I have | we have | I had | we had |
| 2. you have | you have | you had | you had |
| 3. he has | they have | he had | they had |
| she has | | she had | |
| it has | | it had | |

In the future tense the base form *have* is combined with *will* for all subjects, singular and plural.

We **will have** a good time on vacation next summer.

Remember that *have* is one of the most important helping verbs. In the next section you will see that some main verbs require special spellings when they are combined with this helping verb.

## • OTHER IRREGULAR VERBS

There are some other irregular verbs that are used very often. These verbs *do* add *s* or *es* after *he* or *she* or a singular noun in the present tense, but they *do not* add *ed* to form the past tense. This is one of the things that makes them irregular.

On the next page you see a listing of some irregular verbs. Notice that some of these verbs have special spellings when they follow the helping verbs *have, has,* or *had.*

- ## OTHER IRREGULAR VERBS (CONTINUED)

| PRESENT | PAST | PAST after *have*, *has*, *had* |
|---------|------|-------------------------------|
| begin | began | begun |
| bring | brought | brought |
| come | came | come |
| do (does) | did | done |
| drive | drove | driven |
| eat | ate | eaten |
| fly | flew | flown |
| give | gave | given |
| go | went | gone |
| grow | grew | grown |
| make | made | made |
| ride | rode | ridden |
| run | ran | run |
| see | saw | seen |
| sing | sang | sung |
| sink | sank | sunk |
| swim | swam | swum |
| take | took | taken |
| think | thought | thought |
| throw | threw | thrown |
| write | wrote | written |

The verb *do* is spelled *does* after *he* or *she* or a singular noun and the verb *go* is spelled *goes*. The verb *fly* changes to *flies*. All the other verbs add **s** in the present tense.

All these irregular verbs form the **future tense** by adding the word *will* before the basic verb.

We **will be** there soon.

They **will do** what they can.

You **will see** them tomorrow.

I **will go** to the store this afternoon.

# WORDS OFTEN CONFUSED

Some words may *look or sound **almost** the same*, but they have very *different meanings*. Be careful with the spelling of the word you intend to use. Here are some words that sound or look almost the same:

| | | |
|---|---|---|
| than, then | of, off | wonder, wander |
| win, when | who, how | now, know |
| wear, where | our, are | were, where |

These sentences use some of these pairs of words:

I **wonder** where he went. I hope he didn't **wander** away and get lost.

We **were** planning to go to the beach on Saturday. **Where** were you planning to go?

We **are** sure he will arrive before noon. He is one of **our** best friends.

One **of** the eggs rolled **off** the table.

**Who** called on the phone? **How** do you know?

## CHAPTER 1: SENTENCES

### ANSWERS TO QUESTIONS ON PAGE 12.

## Writing Complete Sentences

**1.** YES indicates complete sentences; NO indicates sentences that are not complete.

    1. One of my favorite sports is golf. **YES**

    2. When we can't ride the horses by ourselves. **NO**

    3. They were sitting around watching the news. **YES**

    4. because it helps kids to learn. **NO**

**2.** These answers show the changes or additions needed to write complete sentences. (Answers to each question will vary. Suggested answers are given in boldface.)

    1. When I grow up I **want to be** a football player.

    2. **I couldn't** find them anywhere in my closet.

    3. My family and I **went** to California last summer.

    4. I like to watch TV or play ball.

       (OR: I like to play ball or watch TV.)

**3.** In these answers a word is added to make each sentence complete. (Answers to each question will vary. Suggested answers are given in boldface. People's names can be used instead of pronouns in Numbers 1 and 3. )

    1. **I (She, He)** was surprised to see them

    2. The students were **playing (running)** on the playground.

    3. **We (He, She, They)** looked under the bed and in the closet.

    4. He can **run (swim, talk)** faster than anybody I know.

# CHAPTER 1: SENTENCES

**ANSWERS TO QUESTIONS ON PAGE 13.**

## The Subect of the Sentence

**1.** A short line is drawn after the complete subject.

    1. Sometimes our dog | roams all over the neighborhood.

    2. Once a girl named Stacie | stayed at a hotel with her parents.

    3. Tony and I | wanted to go downtown after school.

    4. Our soccer team | is in second place.

    5. My best friend | rides the bus with me.

**2.** The complete subject is written, and the simple subject is underlined.

    1. <u>I</u>

    2. The <u>people</u> next door

    3. Many <u>ships</u>

    4. Three <u>planes</u>

    5. One large <u>truck</u>

**3.** The complete subject is underlined in those sentences that are complete. A subject has been added in those sentences that were not complete. (Added words are shown in boldface. Answers to Numbers 2, 3, and 5 will vary.)

    1. <u>The game</u> lasted longer than I thought it would.

    2. **My friend** wrote a secret message in the book.

    3. **Today** is the coldest day in years.

    4. <u>She</u> felt better after the snow stopped.

    5. **Our teacher** found the gerbil in the heater pipe.

# CHAPTER 1: SENTENCES

**ANSWERS TO QUESTIONS ON PAGE 14.**

## The Predicate of the Sentence

**1.** A simple predicate is added to each sentence. (Answers to questions will vary. Some possible answers are given in boldface.)

    1. Then he **went (ran, walked)** outside to get some fresh air.

    2. Julie and I **waited (stood)** in line for our turn.

    3. In the magic jungle there **lived (was)** a unicorn.

    4. The next day he **tried** to dig under the wall.

    5. Sometimes she **takes** me bowling or skating.

**2.** The complete predicate is underlined, and another line is added under the word that is the simple predicate.

    1. This fish <u>is much larger than the others</u>.

    2. One day he <u>decided to run away</u>.

    3. My neighbors <u>had an old dog named Ralph</u>.

    4. The scientists <u>analyzed the slimy stuff</u>.

    5. I <u>got a bad sunburn at the beach</u>.

# CHAPTER 1: SENTENCES

**ANSWERS TO QUESTIONS ON PAGE 15.**

## Declarative and Interrogative Sentences

1. Each statement has been rewritten to become a question, and each question has been rewritten to become a statement.

    1. Will she go to camp next summer?

    2. Will the game be played on Monday?

    3. They did hear the thunderstorm last night.

    4. Do they like to read adventure stories?

    5. Erica will carry these packages into the house.

2. The signal words *who, what, when, why, how* have been used to change each statement to a question.

    1. **When** will they come back?

    2. **How** did he hurt his arm?

    3. **Who** were the last ones to leave?

    4. **What** do you want to be when you grow up?

    5. **Why** did the table fall over?

# CHAPTER 1: SENTENCES

**ANSWERS TO QUESTIONS ON PAGE 16.**

## Imperative and Exclamatory Sentences

**1.** A capital letter has been added at the beginning and the correct marks have been added at the end of each sentence.

1. That was the most fun I ever had!

2. Tell me how you figured that out.

3. What an incredible catch that was!

4. He was the greatest ball player I ever saw!

**2.** Each simple statement has been rewritten so that it becomes an exclamation. (Answers will vary.)

1. You can't imagine how hard the rain was falling!

2. We couldn't believe our eyes!

3. You wouldn't believe how hard the wind and snow were blowing!

4. I can't find my shoes anywhere!

**3.** Each question has been rewritten to become a command.

1. Please find the answer to this question.

2. Find out how long we have to wait.

3. Tell me how you got that answer.

4. Please answer the phone.

## Chapter 2: Nouns

### Answers to questions on page 34.

## Using Nouns

**1.** These nouns were listed:

>  carpenter    photograph    dentist    medicine    science

Each of the following sentences uses one of these nouns.

> 1. This **photograph** is fuzzy and blurred.
>
> 2. **Science** is the study of things in nature.
>
> 3. The **carpenter** is making new cabinets and shelves.
>
> 4. I have an appointment to go to the **dentist** tomorrow.
>
> 5. The new **medicine** helped get rid of my cough.

**2.** A noun was printed in boldface in each of the following sentences. These sentences are here rewritten with some *other* nouns that fit.

> 1. My **rabbit (mouse, cat, dog)** is a very good pet.
>
> 2. Does your **sister (mother, father)** like to eat broccoli?
>
> 3. I can't believe you actually like **turtles (snails)**!
>
> 4. They got lost on the way to the **zoo (car, store)**.
>
> 5. Is this your **shoe (hat, glove)** under the bed?

**3.** In these sentences each noun is written and labeled to show its use to name a person, a place, or a thing.

> 1. This sandwich tastes like cardboard!
>     sandwich (thing)  cardboard (thing)
> 2. His brother and her uncle are good friends.
>     brother (person)  uncle (person)  friends (people)
> 3. The carriage traveled from the small town to the city.
>     carriage (thing)  town (place)  city (place)
> 4. Is that a crocodile or an alligator?
>     crocodile (thing)  alligator (thing)
> 5. The detective and his assistant solved the mystery.
>     detective (person) assistant (person) mystery (thing)

# CHAPTER 2: NOUNS

**ANSWERS TO QUESTIONS ON PAGE 35.**

## Singular and Plural Nouns

1. All the nouns in each of these sentences are written separately. There is also an indication of whether each noun is **singular** or **plural**. Here is an example:

> Are my books on the table or on the chair?
> books (plural)   table (singular)  chair (singular)

> 1. The wheels on all these bicycles are bent.
>    wheels (plural)  bicycles (plural)
> 2. My cousin and his friends drove across the country.
>    cousin (singular)  friends (plural) country (singular)
> 3. This sweater is big enough to fit an elephant!
>    sweater (singular)  elephant (singular)
> 4. Chipmunks and squirrels ran through the forest.
>    chipmunks (plural) squirrels (plural) forest (singular)

2. This list of singular nouns was provided:

> story     flashlight     closet     turkey     hamburger

   The following sentences use the **plural** form of one of these nouns in each blank space. (Answers are in boldface.)

> 1. That is the noisiest bunch of **turkeys** I ever heard!
>
> 2. Does this house have many **closets**?
>
> 3. Some of these **hamburgers** are not well cooked.
>
> 4. Both **flashlights** need new batteries.
>
> 5. Have you read all the **stories** in this book?

3. A list of singular and plural nouns was given. Each singular noun is written here in its **plural** form, and each plural noun is written here in its **singular** form.

> 1. sentences     4. customer     7. copies
>
> 2. mysteries     5. prairies     8. audience
>
> 3. chimneys     6. shoulder     9. firemen

# CHAPTER 2: NOUNS

**ANSWERS TO QUESTIONS ON PAGE 36.**

## Common and Proper Nouns

1. A **proper noun** is added at the end of each sentence to complete the statement. All important words in the proper noun should be capitalized. Obviously each student will answer in his or her own way.

   1. My best friend is **Squidley Flemmer.**

   2. A place I would like to visit is **Disneyland.**

   3. The hottest month in summer is **July.**

   4. The busiest street in town is **First Avenue.**

   5. I live in the state of **Iowa.**

2. A list of nouns was given. The necessary capital letters are added to show that each of these is a **proper noun**.

   1. Mississippi River          6. Japan

   2. Saturday                    7. November

   3. England                     8. Mark Twain

   4. Main Street                 9. Denver

   5. Arizona                     10. United States of America

3. Any necessary capital letters are added, and a period or question mark is placed at the end of each sentence.

   1. The states of **A**laska and **T**exas are very large.

   2. My friends went to **W**ashington and **N**ew **Y**ork at **C**hristmas.

   3. Have you ever seen **Y**ellowstone **P**ark or the **G**rand **C**anyon?

   4. We flew across the **P**acific **O**cean to **H**awaii.

   5. Are **G**ermany and **S**pain both in **E**urope?

# CHAPTER 2: NOUNS

**ANSWERS TO QUESTIONS ON PAGE 37.**

## Possessive Nouns

**1.** An **apostrophe** is added to show that **singular possessive nouns** are being used.

    1. I finally found my **dog's** collar.

    2. Where is your **cousin's** house?

    3. The game is at my **sister's** school.

    4. Is this your **friend's** bicycle?

    5. **Frank's** parents came to the meeting.

**2.** The **'s** is added to form a **singular possessive noun** for each word in boldface.

    1. The **lion's** roar scared everybody at the zoo.

    2. I found my **brother's** shoe under the chair.

    3. Is **Mike's** bicycle still out in the rain?

    4. This is the **girl's** camera.

    5. When did **Kim's** sister arrive in town?

**3.** The apostrophe is added to the plural nouns in boldface to show that they are **plural possessive nouns**.

    1. All of my **neighbors'** yards are full of leaves.

    2. The **children's** parents are visiting their school.

    3. Are those the **players'** caps and uniforms?

    4. All of my **sisters'** friends came to visit at the same time.

    5. The **women's** coats are piled on my bed.

# CHAPTER 2: NOUNS

**ANSWERS TO QUESTIONS ON PAGE 38.**

## The Pronouns *I, me, you, we, us*

**1.** Each sentence is rewritten to correct mistakes in the use of pronouns. (Corrections are written in boldface.)

  1. **John and I** are good friends.

  2. They gave gifts to my sister and **me**.

  3. May Alice and **I** go out to play?

  4. My brother and **I** went to the movie together.

  5. They were looking for Ted and Evan and **me**.

**2.** The pronoun *I* is added in the subject part of the sentence. The pronoun *me* is added in the predicate part of the sentence.

  1. My little brother followed **me** on his skateboard.

  2. My dog and **I** do lots of things together.

  3. Mom asked **me** to clean up my room.

  4. **I** finished my work before the bell rang.

  5. Lisa and **I** have been friends since last year.

**3.** The pronouns *we* and *us* are added where blank spaces were indicated.

  1. Tom and I are friends, and **we** spend a lot of time together.

  2. **We** ride our bikes and play ball almost every day.

  3. Our parents gave **us** new baseballs and bats.

  4. When **we** play together, **we** argue a lot.

  5. Nothing will keep **us** from being good friends.

# CHAPTER 2: NOUNS

**ANSWERS TO QUESTIONS ON PAGE 39.**

## The Pronouns *he, she, it, him, her, them, they*

1. The pronouns *he, she,* or *it* are used in place of the nouns that were written in boldface in the original sentences.

    1. **He** will be back soon.

    2. **It** has two flat tires.

    3. **She** is on the playground now.

    4. **It** is falling apart.

    5. **She** looked for colored leaves in the fall.

2. The pronouns *him* or *her* or *it* are used in place of the nouns that are printed in boldface in the original sentences.

    1. I made a phone call to **him**.

    2. Please put **it** on the table

    3. Can you meet **her** this afternoon?

    4. I gave **him** a piece of birthday cake.

    5. Have you looked everywhere for **it**?

3. The subject pronoun *they* replaces nouns that were used as subjects in the original sentences. The object pronoun *them* replaces nouns that were used as objects in the predicate part of the original sentences.

    1. **They** are taking the test now.

    2. I saw **them** at the store yesterday.

    3. **They** were playing on the couch.

    4. When will **they** finish shoveling the snow?

    5. I will ask **them** when they want to leave.

# CHAPTER 2: NOUNS

**ANSWERS TO QUESTIONS ON PAGE 40.**

## Possessive Pronouns

**1.** The **possessive pronoun** is underlined in each sentence.

    1. <u>Which</u> story is your favorite?

    2. All of <u>his</u> balloons have exploded.

    3. Did you see <u>my</u> green umbrella anywhere?

    4. I can't believe <u>her</u> hair is so long.

    5. <u>Their</u> shoes got awfully muddy.

**2.** A **possessive pronoun** is used in each blank space in the original sentences Here is an example:

    He is still looking for ___ keys.
    He is still looking for **his** keys.

    1. Have you finished **your** lunch yet?

    2. They don't seem to know where **their** luggage is.

    3. This toy car doesn't have all **its** wheels.

    4. She is trying to find **her** pencil and paper.

    5. How much did they pay for **their** new car?

# CHAPTER 3: VERBS

### ANSWERS TO QUESTIONS ON PAGE 62.

## Recognizing Verbs

**1.** The *verb* is underlined in each sentence.

   1. The wind <u>scattered</u> the leaves all over the yard.

   2. She <u>celebrates</u> her birthday today.

   3. The house <u>shakes</u> in bad storms.

   4. My teeth <u>chatter</u> in cold weather.

   5. Can you <u>pronounce</u> these words?

**2.** This list of verbs was given:

   perform   describe   prepare   complain   spend

One of these verbs was used in each blank space provided in the original sentences. (Answers are in boldface.)

   1. Does he always **complain** when he falls in the mud?

   2. Try not to **spend** all the money in one place.

   3. Can you **describe** the way he looked?

   4. I must **prepare** for the test tomorrow.

   5. We will **perform** in the school play next week.

# CHAPTER 3: VERBS

**ANSWERS TO QUESTIONS ON PAGE 63.**

## Verbs in the Present Tense

**1.** The correct form of the verb is added in the blank space. Here is an example:

> I watch. He _____. (He **watches**.)

> 1. You wish. She _____. (She **wishes**.)

> 2. They catch. He _____. (He **catches**.)

> 3. I cough. He _____. (He **coughs**.)

> 4. We buy. They _____. (They **buy**.)

> 5. She arrives. You _____. (You **arrive**.)

**2.** Each sentence uses the correct form of the verbs given in parentheses.

> 1. My pet monster **calls** me all sorts of names.

> 2. You **run** faster than Tom's turtle does.

> 3. Ann **pushes** her little sister in the swing.

> 4. Felix **watches** baseball games on TV.

> 5. Ellen **understands** this better than I do.

**3.** Each sentence uses the verb that makes the most sense from the choice provided. The inflections *s* or *es* are added to the verb if they are needed.

> 1. He **hurries** across the busy street.

> 2. She **knows** the answers to most of these questions.

> 3. Joan **visits** her grandparents every summer.

> 4. I often **swim** in the pool near my house.

> 5. Her father **flies** a jet airplane.

# CHAPTER 3: VERBS

**ANSWERS TO QUESTIONS ON PAGE 64.**

## Verbs in the Past Tense

1. Each verb is changed to the **past tense**, and the change is explained. Here is an example:

   carry - change *y* to *i* and add *ed:* **carried**.

   1. smile - drop the final *e* and add *ed:* **smiled**

   2. marry- change *y* to *i* and add *ed:* **married**

   3. discover - add *ed:* **discovered**

   4. bury - change *y* to *i* and add *ed:* **buried**

   5. plan - double the final consonant and add *ed:* **planned**

   6. rescue - drop the final *e* and add *ed:* **rescued**

2. In each sentence the verb in the **past tense** is underlined.

   1. We <u>wondered</u> when the storm would stop.

   2. They <u>continued</u> their work after the game was over.

   3. He <u>worried</u> all day about the test.

   4. Debbie and I <u>waited</u> for Andy to call.

   5. She <u>believed</u> that she would find her lost poodle.

3. Each verb was given in its base form in the original sentences. Here the verb is changed so that it will be in the **past tense**.

   1. We **hurried** home from school yesterday.

   2. They **stopped** the game because of the weather.

   3. The hamster **raced** around in his cage last night.

   4. We **carried** as many books as we could.

   5. Erica **described** what happened yesterday.

# CHAPTER 3: VERBS

**ANSWERS TO QUESTIONS ON PAGE 65.**

## The Irregular Verbs *be* and *have*

**1.** The correct form of the verb **be** is used in each blank space provided in the original sentences.

> 1. Yesterday I **was** outside playing in the leaves.
>
> 2. Today she **is** one of my best friends.
>
> 3. Earlier, my friends **were** in the next room.
>
> 4. Now he **is** upstairs looking for his frog.

**2.** The correct form of the verb **have** is used in each blank space provided in the original sentences. The **present tense** or the **past tense** is used as indicated by the wording of the sentence.

> 1. Today I **have** a lot of homework to do.
>
> 2. Yesterday they **had** a good time at the zoo.
>
> 3. Last week you **had** good luck when you found your money.
>
> 4. Now Sue **has** the bike she always wanted.

**3.** The mistakes in the use of the verbs **be** and **have** are corrected.

> 1. I **have** more work than I can finish.
>
> 2. She **is** not as good at math as I am.
>
> 3. You **were** the first one to see them.
>
> 4. John **has** many different kinds of notebooks.
>
> 5. They **were** upstairs playing with the dragon.

# CHAPTER 3: VERBS

### ANSWERS TO QUESTIONS ON PAGE 66.

## Irregular Verbs in the Past Tense

**1.** Each of the original sentences contained a verb in its base form. This verb is used in the **past tense** in each sentence. Here is an example:

> I **see** the snow fall. I **saw** the snow fall.

1. John **did** his homework before dinner last night.

2. Tina's pet rock **ran** away from home again.

3. She **gave** a party for her scout troop last Saturday.

4. We **bought** new shoes for my brother and his pet camel.

5. You **went** to the park last Saturday, didn't you?

**2.** Here is a list of verbs in their base forms:

> say     come     take     go     see

One of these verbs is used in the **past tense** to fill in the blank provided in each original sentence.

1. We **saw** the wind blow the old tree down last night.

2. My friends **came** to visit me last week.

3. They **said** the package would arrive yesterday.

4. Tom and Ann **took** their little brother to the mall yesterday.

5. We **went** to California on vacation last summer.

**3.** Each sentence is written so that the verb is in the **past tense**.

1. Who **brought** these cookies?

2. I know we **bought** more potato chips than this.

3. She **said** we could play with the gopher.

4. We **sold** lots of lemonade last week when it was hot.

# CHAPTER 3: VERBS

**ANSWERS TO QUESTIONS ON PAGE 67.**

## Verbs in the Future Tense

1. Each verb is written in the present tense. Then the same verb is written in the **past tense** and the **future tense**.

   | | PRESENT | PAST | FUTURE |
   |---|---|---|---|
   | 1. | We see. | We **saw**. | We **will see**. |
   | 2. | They run. | They **ran**. | They **will run**. |
   | 3. | I do. | I **did**. | I **will do**. |
   | 4. | You buy. | You **bought**. | You **will buy**. |
   | 5. | She is. | She **was**. | She **will be**. |

2. This list of verbs was given:   tell   give   run   stop
   One verb from the list is used in the **future tense** in each of these sentences.

   1. I **will give** you some of my cake at lunchtime.

   2. They **will run** in the race tomorrow.

   3. The bus **will stop** at the next corner.

   4. John **will tell** us the story he just heard.

3. Each verb was in the past tense in the original sentences. Now the verb is changed to the **future tense**. Here is an example:

   We dropped all the mirrors. We **will drop** all the mirrors.

   1. We **will see** a movie about teenage mutant ninja turkeys.

   2. He **will go** to the mall with his friends.

   3. They **will shop** for a new doghouse.

   4. My cat **will watch** for the postman.

   5. She **will fall** seven times on the ice.

# CHAPTER 3: VERBS

**ANSWERS TO QUESTIONS ON PAGE 68.**

## Helping Verbs

**1.** Each sentence uses the correct **helping verb** from those shown in parentheses in the original sentences.

1. I **have** eaten twelve bananas.

2. I **have** called three times already.

3. She **has** looked everywhere for her scarf.

4. We **have** written three letters to them.

5. It **has** rained every day this week.

**2.** The correct helping verb *have* or *has* is added in each blank space provided in the original sentences.

1. He **has** played ball with them all summer.

2. I **have** walked up and down the street for an hour.

3. John and Mark **have** been friends all week.

4. Maria **has** painted a beautiful picture.

5. We **have** written letters to our friends.

# CHAPTER 4: ADJECTIVES AND ADVERBS

**ANSWERS TO QUESTIONS ON PAGE 89.**

## Recognizing Adjectives

**1.** All the adjectives in each sentence are underlined, and an arrow is drawn from each adjective to the noun it modifies.

    1. That was an <u>easy</u> test.

    2. He ate <u>four</u> bananas, <u>two</u> pizzas, and <u>an</u> apple.

    3. This <u>little</u> hamster is my <u>favorite</u> animal.

    4. The <u>purple</u> socks don't match your <u>pink</u> shoes.

    5. I like the <u>gray</u> cat better than the <u>brown</u> dog.

**2.** One of these adjectives is used to fit each blank space in the original sentences.

        happy     difficult     eleven     easy     foolish

    1. That was a **foolish** mistake to make.

    2. There are **eleven** players on a football team.

    3. She was **happy** to see her cousin for a visit.

    4. It was not an **easy** test, but I passed it.

    5. That was a very **difficult** problem to figure out.

**3.** Mistakes are corrected in boldface in these sentences.

    1. They gave me **an** extra piece of candy.

    2. She had **an** apple and he had **an** egg.

    3. He drove **an** old rusty car.

    4. We found exactly **the** book we wanted.

    5. We asked **an** assistant to help us.

# CHAPTER 4: ADJECTIVES AND ADVERBS

**ANSWERS TO QUESTIONS ON PAGE 90.**

## Adjectives Ending with *er* and *est*

**1.** Each adjective is followed by the spellings with the *er* and *est* endings. Here is an example:

> sleepy, sleepier, sleepiest

    1. wide, wider, widest         5. light, lighter, lightest

    2. busy, busier, busiest         6. steady, steadier, steadiest

    3. rough, rougher, roughest    7. calm, calmer, calmest

    4. lazy, lazier, laziest         8. noisy, noisier, noisiest

**2.** Adjectives that compare two or more things are underlined.

    1. That was the <u>luckiest</u> catch I ever made.

    2. Erica's parakeet has <u>brighter</u> feathers than mine.

    3. The purple kangaroo is the <u>strangest</u> animal in the zoo.

    4. We caught a <u>larger</u> number of fish than they did.

    5. Have you ever seen a <u>happier</u> group of tadpoles?

**3.** The endings *er* or *est* are added to the adjectives in boldface.

    1. This box is much **heavier** than that one.

    2. His cat has a **thicker** coat than mine does.

    3. She jumped from the **highest** diving board at the pool.

    4. My sister is **younger** than I am.

    5. That is the **fanciest** hat I ever saw.

# CHAPTER 4: ADJECTIVES AND ADVERBS

ANSWERS TO QUESTIONS ON PAGE 91.

## More about Adjectives

**1.** Each of the following adjectives is followed by the forms that compare two things and more than two things. Here is an example:

helpful, more helpful, most helpful

1. interesting, more interesting, most interesting

2. beautiful, more beautiful, most beautiful

3. definite, more definite, most definite

4. remarkable, more remarkable, most remarkable

5. handsome, more handsome, most handsome

6. friendly, more friendly, most friendly

**2.** The **proper adjective** is underlined in each sentence.

1. The English language is spoken in many countries.

2. Alaskan winters are long and cold.

3. Their French poodle is still a puppy.

4. The Canadian border separates Canada from America.

5. She got a Siamese kitten for Christmas.

**3.** The correct form of each adjective in boldface is used.

1. That was the **worst** movie I ever saw.

2. John was **luckier** than I was.

3. Your hot dog tasted **better** than mine.

4. Do you have an **easier** puzzle than this one?

5. It was the **strangest** story I ever read.

# CHAPTER 4: ADJECTIVES AND ADVERBS

### ANSWERS TO QUESTIONS ON PAGE 92.

## Adverbs

**1.** The **adverb** is underlined in each sentence, and an arrow is drawn from the adverb to the verb it describes. Here is an example:

Fred's pet frog rested <u>comfortably</u> on the radiator.

1. The boat <u>finally</u> stopped rocking up and down.

2. We looked <u>outside</u> for the missing gloves.

3. The audience clapped <u>loudly</u> after the concert.

4. The crowd cheered <u>wildly</u> when he hit a home run.

5. Their pet zebra <u>slowly</u> ate five watermelons.

**2.** This list of adverbs was given:

yesterday    carefully    quickly    usually    already

The adverb that fits the blank space in the original sentences is given here in boldface:

1. We walked **quickly** to get out of the rain and wind.

2. They are **usually** home from school before three o'clock.

3. My friends left **yesterday** for their trip back home.

4. They had **already** finished before we got there.

5. Pam **carefully** picked up the broken glass.

# CHAPTER 5: WORD STUDY

### ANSWERS TO QUESTIONS ON PAGE 124.

## Homophones

1. **Homophones** (in boldface) are given to match each word in the original list.

   1. see, **sea**          5. right, **write**

   2. break, **brake**          6. no, **know**

   3. nose, **knows**          7. by, **buy**

   4. eye, **I**          8. peace, **piece**

2. The correct form of the homophones (given in parentheses in the original) is written in boldface.

   1. There is enough space for **two** more people.

   2. We **ate** at a restaurant last night.

   3. The weather report says **it's** going to snow tonight.

   4. I couldn't **hear** what he said.

3. The correct form of the homophone is given in boldface.

   1. Look **through** these books for a picture of a dinosaur.

   2. I **would** like a few more peanuts.

   3. Mike and Ann left **their** books on the bus.

   4. I know **it's** around here somewhere.

# CHAPTER 5: WORD STUDY

**ANSWERS TO QUESTIONS ON PAGE 125.**

## Compound Words

**1.** These words were given:

finger   earth   coat   shoe   news   cheer   water   day   book

One of these words is joined to each of the words in this list to form a new **compound word**.

1. **cheer**leader    4. **news**paper    7. note**book**

2. **water**fall       5. rain**coat**      8. **earth**quake

3. birth**day**        6. **finger**print   9. snow**shoe**

**2.** Correct spelling for these compound words is given.

1. guinea pig    4. no one

2. ice cream    5. all right

3. baby-sitter   6. twenty-seven

**3.** One of these compound words is used in each blank space in the following sentences:

homework   hide-and-seek   all right   haircut

1. I hope you will feel **all right** in the morning.

2. They are playing **hide-and-seek** in the park.

3. Why did she get such a short **haircut**?

4. I finished my **homework** before it got dark.

243

# CHAPTER 5: WORD STUDY
### ANSWERS TO QUESTIONS ON PAGE 126.

## Prefixes and Suffixes

**1.** Each word that begins with a **prefix** is underlined.

> 1. This is an <u>un</u>usual story.
>
> 2. I don't know how all my socks could <u>dis</u>appear.
>
> 3. They will <u>re</u>play the last two minutes of the game.
>
> 4. It took a long time to <u>un</u>load all the bricks.

**2.** Each word written in boldface has a **suffix** added to make it fit the sentence. Here is an example:

> The **win** of the race was very happy.
> The **winner** of the race was very happy.

> 1. They are both very good **swimmers**.
>
> 2. Our **visitor** will stay with us for two days.
>
> 3. Our team **finally** won a game.
>
> 4. The storm blew up very **suddenly**.

**3.** Each word that begins with a **prefix** or ends with a **suffix** is underlined.

> 1. Some <u>read**ers** dis</u>agree with this <u>writ**er**</u>.
>
> 2. <u>Fortunate**ly**</u> they found all their money.
>
> 3. The <u>teach**ers**</u> were <u>help**ful**</u> to all of us.
>
> 4. They rowed <u>quick**ly**</u> back to shore.

# CHAPTER 5: WORD STUDY

### ANSWERS TO QUESTIONS ON PAGE 127.

## Synonyms and Antonyms

**1.** Pairs of words are marked **synonyms** or **antonyms**.

1. light, heavy **antonyms**     4. tired, sleepy **synonyms**

2. shiny, bright **synonyms**     5. before, after **antonyms**

3. above, below **antonyms**     6. start, begin **synonyms**

**2.** One of these words is used as a **synonym** to replace the words in boldface in the original sentences.

skinny     chilly     frightened     breezy

1. It is a very **breezy** day.

2. The new calf has very **skinny** legs.

3. We were **frightened** when we listened to the ghost story.

4. It is very **chilly** this evening.

**3.** One of these words is used as an **antonym** to replace the word in boldface in each of the original sentences.

awake     difficult     closed     soggy

1. It was **difficult** to find all the keys he dropped.

2. This pizza crust is very **soggy.**

3. Please keep the door **closed.**

4. Is everyone **awake?**

# CHAPTER 5: WORD STUDY

### ANSWERS TO QUESTIONS ON PAGE 128.

## Words Often Confused

**1.** The correct word is chosen from the pair of words in parentheses in the original sentences.

> 1. This is **our** first trip to Chicago.
>
> 2. This stone is bigger **than** that one.
>
> 3. They said they had **a lot** of fun at the zoo.
>
> 4. The books all fell **off** the table.
>
> 5. I don't know **where** I left my books.

**2.** These pairs of words are given:

> now, know          an, and          own, won          wonder, wander

The correct word is chosen to fit the blank space given in the original sentences.

> 1. I like to **wander** through the forest when the leaves fall.
>
> 2. Do you **know** how many cookies are left?
>
> 3. We saw the giraffe **and** the elephant at the zoo.
>
> 4. We **won** the game by two points.
>
> 5. I would like to have **an** apple and a banana.

# CHAPTER 5: WORD STUDY

**ANSWERS TO QUESTIONS ON PAGE 129.**

## Contractions

**1.** A contraction is used in place of the words given in boldface in the original sentences.

      1. **We're** going to Chicago on Saturday.

      2. **He's** one of the best players on the team.

      3. **She'll** let us know when we should come.

      4. **They've** gone on a trip.

**2.** A contraction is used in place of the words given in boldface in the original sentences.

      1. I **don't** know when they will arrive.

      2. **Isn't** this an interesting movie?

      3. **Aren't** you finished yet?

      4. He **won't** finish the job until tomorrow.

**3.** The correct contraction is used in place of the word in boldface in the original sentences.

      1. I like kittens. **They're** cute and easy to take care of.

      2. Then he said, "**That's** nice."

      3. You can join even if **you're** only nine.

      4. **She's** very nice and she likes to help children.

# CHAPTER 6: WRITING BETTER SENTENCES

### ANSWERS TO QUESTIONS ON PAGE 156.

## Sentence Fragments

1. The letter **S** indicates that the **sentence** is complete. The letter **F** indicates that the example is only a **fragment**.

> 1. a train trip through the mountains. **F**
>
> 2. Before they got here. **F**
>
> 3. Then I went through a haunted house. **S**
>
> 4. was the day I went to Florida. **F**
>
> 5. I have a little sister and two brothers. **S**

2. Words are added to change the fragments to complete sentences. (Answers will vary. Suggested answers are in boldface.)

> 1. It was very exciting when we **saw Old Faithful erupt**.
>
> 2. **Our teacher** lets us go outside on nice days.
>
> 3. Before school started **I played softball with my friends**.
>
> 4. **My neighbor is** a very close friend to me.
>
> 5. Each year on my summer vacation **I visit my grandmother**.

# CHAPTER 6: WRITING BETTER SENTENCES

### ANSWERS TO QUESTIONS ON PAGE 157.

## Run-on Sentences

1. The letter **S** indicates that the example is a **simple sentence.** The letter **R** indicates that the example is a **run-on sentence**.

   1. My friend is close to me she is my best friend. **R**

   2. One of my favorite sports is golf. **S**

   3. My two cats are both tabby cats they are very cute. **R**

   4. My sister has dark brown hair. **S**

   5. My eyes are blue I like to swim and ride bikes. **R**

2. Each run-on sentence is rewritten as two separate sentences.

   1. I have a dog. I like him a lot.

   2. The storm started at night. The power lines went out.

   3. There was a boy who liked video games. He went to the arcade.

   4. I am nine years old. I want to be a swimming teacher.

   5. My dog doesn't do anything. He just eats and sleeps.

# CHAPTER 6: WRITING BETTER SENTENCES

ANSWERS TO QUESTIONS ON PAGE 158.

## Verb Tenses

1.  The **verb** used in each sentence is rewritten at the end of the sentence, and the words *present, past,* or *future* are used to show the **tense** of the verb.

    1. We hurried to get out of the rain. **hurried** - past

    2. Sometimes the ghost appears out of nowhere. **appears** - present

    3. The game will begin in half an hour. **will begin** - future

    4. The wind blew a lot of leaves into our yard. **blew** - past

    5. We will carry some of these books for you. **will carry** - future

2.  The correct tense is used for each verb originally given in parentheses.

    1. Tomorrow I **will go** to see my grandparents.

    2. Yesterday we **saw** a good program on TV.

    3. Now he **tries** to find the papers he misplaced.

    4. Last summer we **played** baseball almost every day.

    5. Next summer I **will swim** a lot when we go to the beach.

3.  The verb tense is corrected in each example.

    1. Last year my neighbor **had** an old dog named Ralph.

    2. Next week we **will go** for a long drive.

    3. Yesterday I **watched** the storm blow the tree down.

    4. John **looked** for his books for an hour last night.

    5. Tomorrow we **will wash** all the windows.

250

# CHAPTER 6: WRITING BETTER SENTENCES

### ANSWERS TO QUESTIONS ON PAGE 159.

## Using Subject Pronouns and Object Pronouns

**1.** Two pronouns were suggested in each of the original examples. The correct form of each pronoun is used here.

    1. Don said he saw Kevin and **me** yesterday.

    2. **We** are very good friends.

    3. I talked to Bill and **her** yesterday.

    4. **He** and **I** are in the same class.

    5. I hope they will talk to **him** and **me**.

**2.** One **pronoun** is used in place of each word or group of words in boldface in the original sentences. Here is an example:

        **Vera and Pam** are doing their homework.
        **They** are doing their homework.

    1. **She** likes to ride horses.

    2. I saw **them** riding their bikes.

    3. **It** needs some work on its brakes.

    4. **They** were chasing their tails.

    5. **We** are on the same team.

**3.** A blank space was originally included in the second sentence of each pair. Here, a pronoun is used in the blank space. This pronoun refers to the boldface words in the first sentence of each pair.

    1. **I** am working on math. My teacher helps **me.**

    2. **Kim and Lisa** are friends. **They** like the same things.

    3. **Sally** is not here yet. See if you can find **her.**

    4. **My skateboard** is broken. **It** needs a new wheel.

    5. **We** wanted some sandwiches. Mom made some for **us.**

# CHAPTER 6: WRITING BETTER SENTENCES

### ANSWERS TO QUESTIONS ON PAGE 160.

## Compound Subjects, Objects, and Predicates

1. Each pair of sentences is combined into a single sentence with a **compound subject**. Sometimes the form of the verb is changed. Here is an example:

> John **is** in my class. Ellen **is** in my class.
> John and Ellen **are** in my class.

     1. **Ann and I like** chocolate ice cream.

     2. **Mary and Ross are** good student**s**.

     3. **Jim and Don** played after school.

     4. **The dog and the squirrel are** running.

     5. **Kim and Ted have** freckles.

2. Each pair of sentences is combined into a single sentence with a **compound object**. Here is an example:

> I waved to Tom. I waved to Debbie.
> I waved to Tom and Debbie.

     1. Bo plays **baseball and football**.

     2. Joan likes **to swim and ride horses**.

     3. We saw **monkeys and tigers** at the zoo.

     4. You have **a new bike and a new football**.

     5. She is good **at math and spelling**.

# CHAPTER 6: WRITING BETTER SENTENCES

**ANSWERS TO QUESTIONS ON PAGE 161.**

## Compound Subjects, Objects, and Predicates
(continued)

**3.** Each pair of sentences is combined into a single sentence with a **compound predicate**. Here is an example:

> Kate looked in her closet. Kate found her gloves.
> Kate looked in her closet and found her gloves.

1. I **walked** to the store **and bought** some gum.

2. They **raked** the leaves **and cleaned** the gutters.

3. Ann **watched** the sky **and saw** the lightning flash.

4. The dog **found** my shoe **and chewed** it to bits.

5. The car **backed** into the tree **and dented** its bumper.

# CHAPTER 6: WRITING BETTER SENTENCES

**ANSWERS TO QUESTIONS ON PAGE 162.**

## Simple and Compound Sentences

1. The word **simple** is written after each example that is a simple sentence. The word **compound** is written after each example that is a compound sentence.

   1. All my friends like to play basketball. **simple**

   2. We looked under the house, but we found it in the garage. **compound**

   3. Everybody seemed to enjoy the party. **simple**

   4. Giraffes are very large, and they have long necks. **compound**

   5. You can have chocolate cake, or you can have ice cream. **compound**

2. Each pair of simple sentences is rewritten to form a compound sentence using the comma and the word *and*. Here is an example:

   > The snow fell all night. It piled up against the house.
   > The snow fell all night, **and** it piled up against the house.

   1. We went to the park, **and** we saw squirrels and chipmunks.

   2. They traveled all day, **and** they finally got back home.

   3. I tried to solve the puzzle, **and** I finally figured it out.

   4. The wind was blowing very hard, **and** several trees fell down.

   5. I had a birthday party, **and** I asked my friends to come.

# CHAPTER 6: WRITING BETTER SENTENCES

**ANSWERS TO QUESTIONS ON PAGE 163.**

## Simple and Compound Sentences
(continued)

3. Pairs of simple sentences are joined to form compound sentences using the words *but* or *or*.

> 1. I looked for an hour, **but** I couldn't find anything.
>
> 2. Do you want more spaghetti, **or** would you rather have broccoli?
>
> 3. They thought they had the answer, **but** they were mistaken.
>
> 4. You can ride with us, **or** you can take the bus.
>
> 5. We worked hard all day, **but** we didn't finish the job.

# CHAPTER 7: PUNCTUATION

ANSWERS TO QUESTIONS ON PAGE 177.

## Commas

**1.** Commas are used to make these sentences clear to the reader. Periods are also added as needed.

1. We went to Chicago, Illinois, and to Detroit, Michigan.

2. The letter was sent on March 10, 1990.

3. They traveled to Idaho, Montana, and Utah on vacation.

4. Today is Friday, November 2, 1990.

5. I have friends in Buffalo, N.Y., and in Santa Fe, N.M.

**2.** Commas are added as needed, and punctuation is added at the end of each sentence.

1. Yes, I know where he is.

2. John, please tell your parrot to be quiet.

3. No, she hasn't arrived yet.

4. Class, we will be taking a trip tomorrow.

5. Joan, will you see who is at the door?

**3.** Commas separate the series of words in each sentence.

1. Fred, Ann, and Tom were late for the bus.

2. Washington, Oregon, and California are states in the west.

3. My favorite pets are dogs, cats, frogs, and elephants.

4. The weather was mild, pleasant, and sunny.

5. We saw roses, daisies, and marigolds in the flower garden.

# CHAPTER 7: PUNCTUATION

ANSWERS TO QUESTIONS ON PAGE **178.**

## Abbreviations and End Marks

**1.** Capital letters and periods are used to write these names correctly.

1. Mr. John Edwards
2. Miss Ellen White
3. Mrs. Alice Franklin
4. Ms. Janice V. Adams

5. Mr. Allan B. Jones
6. Mrs. A. R. Williams
7. Dr. Thomas Brown
8. Ms. R. Ellen White

**2.** Capital letters are added for the first word and for all the proper nouns as well.

1. Bob and Ellen are going to New York.
2. Mr. and Mrs. Elliott went home for Thanksgiving.
3. What costumes are Sue and Kim wearing for Halloween?
4. California is in the western United States.
5. Have you ever been to Kansas or to Iowa?

**3.** The *abbreviation* that matches each of the first four words is given. The *word* that matches the last four abbreviations is given.

1. Saturday **Sat.**
2. February **Feb.**
3. Wednesday **Wed.**
4. October **Oct.**

5. Sept. **September**
6. Jan. **January**
7. Mon. **Monday**
8. Dr. **Doctor**

# CHAPTER 7: PUNCTUATION

**ANSWERS TO QUESTIONS ON PAGE 179.**

## Abbreviations and End Marks (continued)

**4.** Proper names and abbreviations are corrected, as are the beginning and end of each sentence.

1. The letter was addressed to Mr. Donald R. Jones in Denver.

2. I got back from Houston and Dallas in October.

3. Abraham Lincoln was president during the Civil War.

4. Did they say they were going to Michigan or to Minnesota?

5. I first met Mrs. Smith and Ms. Jones in April of last year.

# CHAPTER 7: PUNCTUATION

**ANSWERS TO QUESTIONS ON PAGE 180.**

## Quotation Marks

**1.** Quotation marks are added to show that someone is speaking in each of these sentences.

> 1. He said, "I will meet you at the movie this afternoon."
>
> 2. "Where has everyone gone?" she asked.
>
> 3. "I don't know where they are," he said.
>
> 4. Then she said, "I will get there as soon as I can."
>
> 5. "I never saw such a big pumpkin!" he exclaimed.

**2.** Quotation marks and commas are added as needed.

> 1. They said, "We can't find our coats or umbrellas."
>
> 2. "How many cookies are left?" she asked.
>
> 3. John said, "We visited my aunt, my cousin, and my grandmother."
>
> 4. "What does your gorilla like to eat?" asked Julie.
>
> 5. "Here are more cookies, cakes, and drinks," said Mom.

# INDEX

This index lists all topics discussed in Chapters 1-7.

If you want to find only a brief definition of a term, turn directly to the HANDBOOK FOR QUICK REFERENCE on page 181. There you will see a separate listing that shows where each topic is discussed in the HANDBOOK.

# INDEX

# INDEX

# The
# *Using Your Language*
# Series

*Elementary Grammar: A Child's Resource Book* (1991)

Forthcoming Titles:

*Intermediate Grammar: A Student's Resource Book*

*Elementary Composition: A Child's Resource Book*

*Intermediate Composition: A Student's Resource Book*

The *Using Your Language* series is specially designed to provide young people with home resource books. These guides serve as references in the areas of English grammar and composition. They offer clear explanations of these critical communication skills to students throughout their school careers.

Especially at a time when many schools are offering less comprehensive coverage of the basics, these guides belong in every home reference collection.

**ORDER INFORMATION**— *Check your local bookstore or order by mail.*

To order Grayson Bernard books by mail, fill in the form below and mail to:

Grayson Bernard Publishers
P.O. Box 5247
Dept. G1
Bloomington, IN  47407

---

## ORDER FORM

| | Number of copies | | Price | Total |
|---|---|---|---|---|
| *Elementary Grammar: A Child's Resource Book* | _____ | x | $13.95 | _____ |
| *Help Your Child Read and Succeed: A Parents' Guide* | _____ | x | $12.95 | _____ |

**Sales Tax:**
Please add 5% for books shipped to Indiana addresses.                      _____

**Shipping:**
❏  Book rate: $2.00 for the first book and $1.00 for each additional book.
❏  Air Mail: $3.00 for the first book and $1.50 for each additional book.      _____

**TOTAL**                                                                $ _____
(Please send check or money order.)

Name _____

Address _____

_____Zip _____

❏   Please send the ***Parent** & Child . . . learning together* newsletter to me FREE for a year.

*Your satisfaction is guaranteed.*
Any book may be returned for a full refund—no questions asked.

G1

## GRAYSON BERNARD
### P U B L I S H E R S